WORD BY WORD BASIC

Second Edition

ENGLISH/ SPANISH

DICCIONARIO ILUSTRADO DE INGLÉS

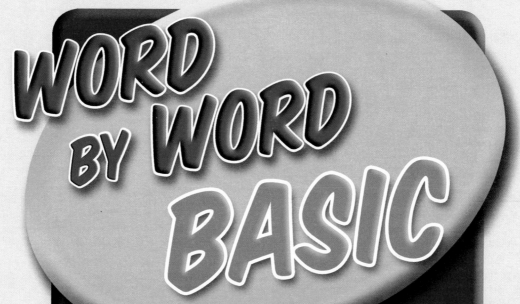

Steven J. Molinsky • Bill Bliss

Herlinda Charpentier Saitz, Translator

Illustrated by
Richard E. Hill

PEARSON
Longman

Word by Word Basic Picture Dictionary, English/Spanish second edition

Pearson Education, 10 Bank Street, White Plains, NY 10606

Editorial director: Pam Fishman
Vice president, director of design and production: Rhea Banker
Director of electronic production: Aliza Greenblatt
Director of manufacturing: Patrice Fraccio
Senior manufacturing manager: Edith Pullman
Director of marketing: Oliva Fernandez
Associate development editor: Mary Perrotta Rich
Senior digital layout specialist: Wendy Wolf
Text design: Wendy Wolf
Cover design: Tracey Munz Cataldo/Warren Fischbach
Realia creation: Warren Fischbach, Paula Williams
Illustrations: Richard E. Hill
Contributing artists: Steven Young, Charles Cawley, Willard Gage, Marlon Violette
Reviewers: Marta E. Luján, The University of Texas at Austin; Carmen Schlig, Georgia State University;
Project management by TransPac Education Services, Victoria, BC, Canada with assistance from
Robert Zacharias, Studio G, & Susa Oñate

Additional photos/illustration: Page **244** *top* U.S. National Archives & Records Administration

ISBN 0-13-148234-3
ISBN 13 9780131482340
Longman on the Web
Longman.com offers online resources for teachers and students. Access our Companion Websites,
our online catalog, and our local offices around the world.

Visit us at longman.com.

Printed in the United States of America
1 2 3 4 5 6 7 8 9 10 – QWD – 12 11 10 09 08 07

Dedicated to Janet Johnston in honor of her
wonderful contribution to the development of
our textbooks over three decades.

Steven J. Molinsky
Bill Bliss

CONTENTS

ÍNDICE/CONTENIDO

Unit / Theme	Communication Skills	Writing & Discussion	CASAS	LAUSD	LCPs
1 **Personal Information and Family**	• Asking for & giving personal information • Identifying information on a form • Spelling name aloud • Identifying family members • Introducing others	• Telling about yourself • Telling about family members • Drawing a family tree	0.1.2, 0.1.4, 0.2.1, 0.2.2	*Beg. Literacy:* 1, 2, 3, 4, 5 *Beg. Low:* 1, 2, 4, 6, 7, 9, 58 *Beg. High:* 1, 4, 5, 6	*Literacy LCPs:* 01, 02, 07, 08, 15, 16 *LCP A:* 05, 14, 15 *LCP B:* 22, 31 *LCP C:* 39
2 **At School**	• Identifying classroom objects • Identifying classroom locations • Identifying classroom actions • Giving & following simple classroom commands • Identifying school locations & personnel	• Describing a classroom • Describing a school • Comparing schools in different countries	0.1.2, 0.1.5	*Beg. Literacy:* 8, 9, 11 *Beg. Low:* 12, 13, 15, 16, 17, 18 *Beg. High:* 12, 14, 15	*Literacy LCPs:* 01, 07, 15
3 **Common Everyday Activities and Language**	• Identifying everyday & leisure activities • Inquiring by phone about a person's activities • Asking about a person's plan for future activities • Social communication: Greeting people, Leave taking, Introducing yourself & others, Getting someone's attention, Expressing gratitude, Saying you don't understand, Calling someone on the telephone • Describing the weather • Interpreting temperatures on a thermometer (Fahrenheit & Centigrade) • Describing the weather forecast for tomorrow	• Making a list of daily activities • Describing daily routine • Making a list of planned activities • Describing favorite leisure activities • Describing the weather	0.1.1, 0.1.2, 0.1.4, 0.1.6, 0.2.1, 0.2.4, 1.1.5, 2.1.8, 2.3.3, 7.5.5, 7.5.6, 8.2.3, 8.2.5	*Beg. Literacy:* 5, 6 *Beg. Low:* 9, 11, 12, 13, 28, 29 *Beg. High:* 7a, 7b, 11, 26	*Literacy LCPs:* 01, 02, 07, 08, 15, 16 *LCP A:* 05, 06, 13 *LCP B:* 22, 30 *LCP C:* 39, 47

CASAS: Comprehensive Adult Student Assessment System
LAUSD: Los Angeles Unified School District content standards *(Beginning Literacy, Beginning Low, Beginning High)*
LCPs: Literacy Completion Points – Florida & Texas workforce development skills & life skills –
    (Literacy levels; LCP A – Literacy/Foundations; LCP B – Low Beginning; LCP C – High Beginning)

Unit / Theme	Communication Skills	Writing & Discussion	CASAS	LAUSD	LCPs
4 Numbers/ Time/ Money/ Calendar	• Using cardinal & ordinal numbers • Giving information about age, number of family members, residence • Telling time • Indicating time of events • Asking for information about arrival & departure times • Identifying coins & currency – names & values • Making & asking for change • Identifying days of the week • Identifying months of the year • Asking about the year, month, day, date • Asking about the date of a birthday, anniversary, appointment • Giving date of birth	• Describing numbers of students in a class • Identifying a country's population • Describing daily schedule with times • Telling about the use of time in different cultures or countries • Describing the cost of purchases • Describing coins & currency of other countries • Describing weekday activities • Telling about favorite day of the week & month of the year	0.1.2, 0.2.1, 1.1.6, 2.3.1, 2.3.2	*Beg. Literacy:* 6, 12, 13 *Beg. Low:* 3, 4, 25, 26, 30 *Beg. High:* 2, 5	*Literacy LCPs:* 01, 03, 07, 09, 15, 17 *LCP A:* 08 *LCP B:* 25 *LCP C:* 42
5 Home	• Identifying types of housing & communities • Requesting a taxi • Calling 911 for an ambulance • Identifying rooms of a home • Identifying furniture • Complimenting • Asking for information in a store • Locating items in a store • Asking about items on sale • Asking the location of items at home • Telling about past weekend activities • Identifying locations in an apartment building • Identifying ways to look for housing: classified ads, listings, vacancy signs • Renting an apartment • Describing household problems • Securing home repair services • Making a suggestion • Identifying household cleaning items • Identifying tools and home supplies • Asking to borrow an item	• Describing types of housing where people live • Describing rooms & furniture in a residence • Telling about baby products & early child-rearing practices in different countries • Telling about personal experiences with repairing things • Describing an apartment building • Describing household cleaning chores	0.1.2, 0.1.4, 1.4.1, 1.4.2, 1.4.7, 2.1.2, 7.5.5, 8.2.5, 8.2.6	*Beg. Low:* 12, 13, 21, 38, 39 *Beg. High:* 10c, 20, 37, 38, 39	*Literacy LCPs:* 01, 07, 11, 15, 19 *LCP A:* 04, 06, 11 *LCP B:* 21 *LCP C:* 38, 40, 45
6 Community	• Identifying places in the community • Exchanging greetings • Asking & giving the location of places in the community • Identifying government buildings, services, & other places in a city/town center • Identifying modes of transportation in a city/town center	• Describing places in a neighborhood • Making a list of places, people, & actions observed at an intersection	0.1.2, 0.1.4, 2.5.3, 2.5.4	*Beg. Literacy:* 5, 11 *Beg. Low:* 22, 23, 24 *Beg. High:* 23	*Literacy LCPs:* 01, 04, 07, 11, 15 *LCP A:* 05, 12 *LCP B:* 29 *LCP C:* 46

Unit / Theme	Communication Skills	Writing & Discussion	CASAS	LAUSD	LCPs
7 Describing	• Describing people by age • Describing people by physical characteristics • Describing a suspect or missing person to a police officer • Describing people & things using adjectives • Describing physical states & emotions • Expressing concern about another person's physical state or emotion	• Describing physical characteristics of yourself & family members • Describing physical characteristics of a favorite actor or actress or other famous person • Describing things at home & in the community • Telling about personal experiences with different emotions	0.1.2, 0.2.1	*Beg. Literacy:* 7 *Beg. Low:* 6 *Beg. High:* 3, 7b	*Literacy LCPs:* 01, 07, 15 *LCP A:* 05 *LCP B:* 22 *LCP C:* 39, 49
8 Food	• Identifying food items (fruits, vegetables, meat, poultry, seafood, dairy products, juices, beverages, deli, frozen foods, snack foods, groceries) • Identifying non-food items purchased in a supermarket (e.g., household supplies, baby products, pet food) • Determining food needs to make a shopping list • Asking the location of items in a supermarket • Identifying supermarket sections • Requesting items at a service counter in a supermarket • Identifying supermarket checkout area personnel & items • Identifying food containers & quantities • Identifying units of measure • Asking for & giving recipe instructions • Complimenting someone on a recipe • Offering to help with food preparation • Identifying food preparation actions • Ordering fast food items, coffee shop items, & sandwiches • Indicating a shortage of supplies to a co-worker or supervisor • Taking customers' orders at a food service counter • Identifying restaurant objects, personnel, & actions • Making & following requests at work • Identifying & correctly positioning silverware & plates in a table setting • Inquiring in person about restaurant job openings • Ordering from a restaurant menu • Taking customers' orders as a waiter or waitress in a restaurant	• Describing favorite & least favorite foods • Describing foods in different countries • Making a shopping list • Describing places to shop for food • Telling about differences between supermarkets & food stores in different countries • Making a list of items in kitchen cabinets & the refrigerator • Describing recycling practices • Describing a favorite recipe using units of measure • Telling about experience with different types of restaurants • Describing restaurants and menus in different countries • Describing favorite foods ordered in restaurants	0.1.2, 0.1.4, 1.1.1, 1.1.7, 1.3.7, 1.3.8, 2.6.4, 4.8.3	*Beg. Literacy:* 5, 14 *Beg. Low:* 14, 32, 35, 37 *Beg. High:* 10c, 30, 31, 34, 36	*Literacy LCPs:* 01, 05, 07, 12, 15, 20 *LCP A:* 05, 07, 11 *LCP B:* 24, 28 *LCP C:* 45

Unit / Theme	Communication Skills	Writing & Discussion	CASAS	LAUSD	LCPs
9 **Colors, Clothing, & Shopping**	• Identifying colors • Complimenting someone on clothing • Identifying clothing items, including outerwear, sleepwear, underwear, exercise clothing, footwear, jewelry, & accessories • Talking about appropriate clothing for different weather conditions • Expressing clothing needs to a store salesperson • Locating clothing items • Inquiring about ownership of found clothing items • Indicating loss of a clothing item • Asking about sale prices in a clothing store • Reporting theft of a clothing item to the police • Stating preferences during clothing shopping • Expressing problems with clothing & the need for alterations • Identifying departments & services in a department store • Asking the location of items in a department store • Asking to buy, return, exchange, try on, & pay for department store items • Asking about regular & sales prices, discounts, & sales tax • Interpreting a sales receipt • Offering assistance to customers as a salesperson • Expressing needs to a salesperson in a store • Identifying electronics products, including video & audio equipment, telephones, cameras, & computers • Identifying components of a computer & common computer software • Complimenting someone about an item & inquiring where it was purchased	• Describing the flags of different countries • Telling about emotions associated with different colors • Telling about clothing & colors you like to wear • Describing clothing worn at different occasions (e.g., going to schools, parties, weddings) • Telling about clothing worn in different weather conditions • Telling about clothing worn during exercise activities • Telling about footwear worn during different activities • Describing the color, size, & pattern of favorite clothing items • Comparing clothing fashions now & a long time ago • Describing a department store • Telling about stores that have sales • Telling about an item purchased on sale • Comparing different types & brands of video & audio equipment, telephones, & cameras • Describing personal use of a computer • Sharing opinions about why computers are important	0.1.2, 0.1.3, 0.1.4, 1.1.9, 1.2.1, 1.2.2, 1.2.3, 1.3.3, 1.3.7, 1.3.9, 1.6.3, 1.6.4, 4.8.3, 8.2.4	*Beg. Literacy:* 5, 8, 13, 14 *Beg. Low:* 14, 31, 32, 33, 34 *Beg. High:* 10c, 30, 33, 60	*Literacy LCPs:* 01, 04, 07, 11, 15, 19 *LCP A:* 05, 11, 15 *LCP B:* 28 *LCP C:* 45

Unit / Theme	Communication Skills	Writing & Discussion	CASAS	LAUSD	LCPs
10 **Community Services**	• Requesting bank services & transactions (e.g., deposit, withdrawal, cashing a check, obtaining traveler's checks, opening an account, applying for a loan, exchanging currency) • Identifying bank personnel • Identifying bank forms • Asking about acceptable forms of payment (cash, check, credit card, money order, traveler's check) • Identifying household bills (rent, utilities, etc.) • Identifying family finance documents & actions • Following instructions to use an ATM machine • Requesting post office services & transactions • Identifying types of mail & mail services • Identifying different ways to buy stamps • Requesting non-mail services available at the post office (money order, selective service registration, passport application) • Identifying & locating library sections, services, & personnel • Asking how to find a book in the library • Identifying community institutions, services, and personnel (police, fire, city government, public works, recreation, sanitation, religious institutions) • Identifying types of emergency vehicles	• Describing use of bank services • Telling about household bills & amounts paid • Telling about the person responsible for household finances • Describing use of ATM machines • Describing use of postal services • Comparing postal systems in different countries • Telling about experience using a library • Telling about the location of community institutions • Describing experiences using community institutions	0.1.2, 1.3.1, 1.3.3, 1.4.4, 1.5.1, 1.5.3, 1.8.1, 1.8.2, 1.8.4, 2.4.1, 2.4.2, 2.4.4, 2.5.1, 2.5.4, 2.5.6, 8.2.1	*Beg. Low:* 8 *Beg. High:* 24, 28, 29	*Literacy LCPs:* 01, 07, 15, 19 *LCP A:* 08, 11, 12 *LCP B:* 25, 28, 29 *LCP C:* 42, 44, 46

Unit / Theme	Communication Skills	Writing & Discussion	CASAS	LAUSD	LCPs
11 **Health**	• Identifying parts of the body & key internal organs • Describing ailments, symptoms, & injuries • Asking about the health of another person • Identifying items in a first-aid kit • Describing medical emergencies • Identifying emergency medical procedures (CPR, rescue breathing, Heimlich maneuver) • Calling 911 to report a medical emergency • Identifying major illnesses • Talking with a friend or co-worker about illness in one's family • Following instructions during a medical examination • Identifying medical personnel, equipment, & supplies in medical & dental offices • Understanding medical & dental personnel's description of procedures during treatment • Understanding a doctor's medical advice and instructions • Identifying over-the-counter medications • Understanding dosage instructions on medicine labels • Identifying hospital departments & personnel • Identifying equipment in a hospital room • Identifying actions & items related to personal hygiene • Locating personal care products in a store • Identifying actions & items related to baby care	• Describing self • Telling about a personal experience with an illness or injury • Describing remedies or treatments for common problems (cold, stomachache, insect bite, hiccups) • Describing experience with a medical emergency • Describing a medical examination • Describing experience with a medical or dental procedure • Telling about medical advice received • Telling about over-the-counter medications used • Comparing use of medications in different countries • Describing a hospital stay • Making a list of personal care items needed for a trip • Comparing baby products in different countries	0.1.2, 0.1.4, 1.3.7, 2.1.2, 2.5.3, 2.5.9, 3.1.1, 3.1.2, 3.1.3, 3.3.1, 3.3.2, 3.3.3, 3.4.2, 3.4.3, 3.5.4, 3.5.5, 3.5.9, 8.1.1	*Beg. Literacy:* 9 *Beg. Low:* 12, 21, 32, 43, 44, 45, 46 *Beg. High:* 10b, 20, 30, 43, 45, 46, 47, 50	*Literacy LCPs:* 01, 05, 06, 07, 12, 14, 15, 20, 22 *LCP A:* 06, 07, 10, 14 *LCP B:* 24, 27 *LCP C:* 40, 41, 44, 48

Unit / Theme	Communication Skills	Writing & Discussion	CASAS	LAUSD	LCPs
12 **School Subjects and Activities**	• Identifying school subjects • Identifying extracurricular activities • Sharing after-school plans • MATH: • Asking & answering basic questions during a math class • Using fractions to indicate sale prices • Using percents to indicate test scores & probability in weather forecasts • Identifying high school math subjects • Using measurement terms to indicate height, width, depth, length, distance • Interpreting metric measurements • Identifying types of lines, geometric shapes, & solid figures • ENGLISH LANGUAGE ARTS: • Identifying types of sentences • Identifying parts of speech • Identifying punctuation marks • Providing feedback during peer-editing • Identifying steps of the writing process • Identifying types of literature • Identifying forms of writing • GEOGRAPHY: • Identifying geographical features & bodies of water • Identifying natural environments (desert, jungle, rainforest, etc.) • SCIENCE: • Identifying science classroom/laboratory equipment • Asking about equipment needed to do a science procedure • Identifying steps of the scientific method	• Telling about favorite school subject • Telling about extracurricular activities • Comparing extracurricular activities in different countries • Describing math education • Telling about something bought on sale • Researching & sharing information about population statistics using percents • Describing favorite books & authors • Describing newspapers & magazines read • Telling about use of different types of written communication • Describing the geography of your country • Describing geographical features experienced • Describing experience with scientific equipment • Describing science education • Brainstorming a science experiment & describing each step of the scientific method	0.1.2, 0.1.3, 0.1.5, 0.2.3, 1.1.2, 1.1.4, 2.5.5, 2.5.9, 2.7.5, 5.2.5, 6.0.1, 6.0.2, 6.0.4, 6.1.1, 6.1.2, 6.1.3, 6.1.4, 6.4.1, 6.4.2, 6.6.1, 6.6.2, 6.8.1	*Beg. Literacy:* 15 *Beg. Low:* 12, 16, 17 *Beg. High:* 7a, 14, 31	*Literacy LCPs:* 01, 07, 15 *LCP A:* 14 *LCP B:* 31 *LCP C:* 39, 48

Unit / Theme	Communication Skills	Writing & Discussion	CASAS	LAUSD	LCPs
13 **Work**	• Identifying occupations • Talking about occupation during social conversation • Identifying job skills & work activities • Indicating job skills during an interview • Identifying types of job advertisements (help wanted signs, job notices, classified ads) • Interpreting abbreviations in job advertisements • Identifying each step in a job-search process • Making requests at work • Identifying factory locations, equipment, & personnel • Asking the location of workplace departments & personnel to orient oneself as a new employee • Asking about the location & activities of a co-worker • Identifying construction site machinery, equipment, and building materials • Asking a co-worker for a workplace item • Warning a co-worker of a safety hazard • Asking whether there is a sufficient supply of workplace materials • Identifying job safety equipment • Interpreting warning signs at work • Reminding someone to use safety equipment • Asking the location of emergency equipment at work	• Career exploration: sharing ideas about occupations that are interesting, difficult, important • Describing occupation & occupations of family members • Describing job skills • Describing a familiar job (skill requirements, qualifications, hours, salary) • Telling about how people found their jobs • Telling about experience with a job search or job interview • Describing a nearby factory & working conditions there • Comparing products produced by factories in different countries • Describing building materials used in ones dwelling • Describing a nearby construction site • Telling about experience with safety equipment • Describing the use of safety equipment in the community	0.1.2, 0.1.6, 4.1.2, 4.1.3, 4.1.5, 4.1.6, 4.1.7, 4.1.8, 4.3.1, 4.3.3, 4.3.4, 4.5.1, 4.6.1, 7.1.1, 7.5.5	*Beg. Literacy:* 5, 10 *Beg. Low:* 11, 12, 14, 48, 49, 50, 51, 52, 53, 54, 56 *Beg. High:* 7a, 8a, 11, 51, 54	*Literacy LCPs:* 01, 07, 10, 14, 15, 18, 22 *LCP A:* 01, 02, 03, 04, 10 *LCP B:* 18, 19, 20, 21, 27 *LCP C:* 35, 36, 38, 44
14 **Transportation and Travel**	• Identifying modes of local & inter-city public transportation • Expressing intended mode of travel • Asking about a location to obtain transportation (bus stop, bus station, train station, subway station) • Locating ticket counters, information booths, fare card machines, & information signage in transportation stations • Giving & following driving directions (using prepositions of motion) • Interpreting traffic signs • Warning a driver about an upcoming sign • Interpreting compass directions • Asking for driving directions • Following instructions during a driver's test • Repeating to confirm instructions • Identifying airport locations & personnel (check-in, security, gate, baggage claim, Customs & Immigration) • Asking for location of places & personnel at an airport • Indicating loss of travel documents or other items	• Describing mode of travel to different places in the community • Describing local public transportation • Comparing transportation in different countries • Describing your route from home to school • Describing how to get to different places from home and school • Describing local traffic signs • Comparing traffic signs in different countries • Describing a familiar airport • Telling about an experience with Customs & Immigration	0.1.2, 0.1.3, 0.1.6, 1.9.1, 1.9.2, 1.9.4, 2.2.1, 2.2.2, 2.2.3, 2.2.4, 2.5.4	*Beg. Literacy:* 5, 10 *Beg. Low:* 11, 13, 23, 24, 42, 48, 49 *Beg. High:* 11, 23, 41	*Literacy LCPs:* 01, 04, 06, 07, 13, 15, 21 *LCP A:* 09 *LCP B:* 26 *LCP C:* 43

Unit / Theme	Communication Skills	Writing & Discussion	CASAS	LAUSD	LCPs
15 **Recreation and Entertainment**	• Identifying places to go for outdoor recreation, entertainment, culture, etc. • Asking for & offering a suggestion for a leisure activity • Describing past weekend activities • Describing activities planned for a future day off or weekend • Identifying individual sports & recreation activities • Asking and telling about favorite sports and recreation activities • Describing exercise habits & routines • Identifying team sports & terms for players & playing fields • Commenting on a player's performance during a game • Engaging in small talk about favorite sports, teams, and players • Identifying types of entertainment & cultural events • Identifying different genres of music, movies, & TV programs • Expressing likes about types of entertainment	• Describing favorite places to go & activities there • Describing favorite individual sports & recreation activities • Comparing individual sports & recreation activities popular in different countries • Describing favorite team sports & famous players • Telling about favorite types of entertainment • Comparing types of entertainment popular in different countries • Telling about favorite performers • Telling about favorite types of music, movies, & TV programs	0.1.2, 0.1.3, 0.1.4, 0.2.4, 2.6.1, 2.6.2, 2.6.3, 2.7.6, 3.5.8, 3.5.9	*Beg. Low:* 12, 13, 14 *Beg. High:* 7a	*Literacy LCPs:* 01, 07, 15 *LCP A:* 05, 06 *LCP C:* 39
16 **U.S. Civics**	• Producing correct form of identification when requested (driver's license, social security card, student I.D. card, employee I.D. badge, permanent resident card, passport, visa, work permit, birth certificate, proof of residence) • Identifying the three branches of U.S. government (legislative, executive, judicial) & their functions • Identifying senators, representatives, the president, vice-president, cabinet, Supreme Court justices, & the chief justice, & the branches of government in which they work • Identifying the key buildings in each branch of government (Capitol Building, White House, Supreme Court Building) • Identifying the Constitution as "the supreme law of the land" • Identifying the Bill of Rights • Naming freedoms guaranteed by the 1st Amendment • Identifying key amendments to the Constitution • Identifying key holidays & dates they occur	• Telling about forms of identification & when needed • Comparing the governments of different countries • Describing how people in a community "exercise their 1st Amendment rights" • Brainstorming ideas for a new amendment to the Constitution • Describing U.S. holidays you celebrate • Describing holidays celebrated in different countries	0.1.2, 0.1.3, 2.7.1, 5.1.6, 5.2.1, 5.2.2, 5.5.2, 5.5.3, 5.5.4	*Beg. Low:* 40 *Beg. High:* 40, 42	*Literacy LCPs:* 01, 07, 15 *LCP A:* 12 *LCP B:* 26, 29 *LCP C:* 43, 46

Welcome to the second edition of the *WORD BY WORD BASIC* Picture Dictionary! This text presents more than 2,500 vocabulary words through vibrant illustrations and simple accessible lesson pages with large type that are designed for clarity and ease-of-use with learners at low-beginning and literacy levels. Our goal is to prepare students for success using English in everyday life, in the community, in school, and at work.

WORD BY WORD BASIC is an abridged version of the "full" *Word by Word* Picture Dictionary. It organizes the vocabulary into 16 thematic units, providing a careful research-based sequence of lessons that integrates students' development of grammar and vocabulary skills through topics that begin with the immediate world of the student and progress to the world at large. Early lessons on the family, the home, and daily activities lead to lessons on the community, school, workplace, shopping, recreation, and other topics. The text offers extensive coverage of important lifeskill competencies and the vocabulary of school subjects and extracurricular activities, and it is designed to meet the objectives of current national, state, and local standards-based curricula you can find in the Scope & Sequence on the previous pages.

Since each lesson in *Word by Word Basic* is self-contained, it can be used either sequentially or in any desired order. For users' convenience, the lessons are listed in two ways: sequentially in the Table of Contents, and alphabetically in the Thematic Index. These resources, combined with the Glossary in the appendix, allow students and teachers to quickly and easily locate all words and topics in the Picture Dictionary.

The *Word by Word Basic* Picture Dictionary is the centerpiece of the complete *Word by Word Basic* Vocabulary Development Program, which offers a wide selection of print and media support materials for instruction at all levels.

A unique choice of workbooks offers flexible options to meet students' needs. A Vocabulary Workbook features motivating vocabulary, grammar, and listening practice. A standards-based Lifeskills Workbook provides competency-based activities and reading tied to national, state, and local curriculum frameworks. A Literacy Workbook offers fundamental practice with the alphabet and basic reading and writing skills for pre-Beginners.

The Teacher's Guide and Lesson Planner with CD-ROM includes lesson-planning suggestions, community tasks, Internet weblinks, and reproducible masters to save teachers hours of lesson preparation time. A Handbook of Vocabulary Teaching Strategies is included in the Teacher's Guide. The CD-ROM contains a complete Activity Bank of reproducible grammar and vocabulary worksheets for each unit and innovative level-specific lesson-planning forms that teachers can fill in and print out for quick and easy lesson preparation.

The Audio Program includes all words and conversations for interactive practice and—as bonus material—an expanded selection of WordSongs for entertaining musical practice with the vocabulary.

Additional ancillary materials include Color Transparencies, Vocabulary Game Cards, a Testing Program, and ExamView CD-ROM. Bilingual Editions are also available.

Teaching Strategies

Word by Word Basic presents vocabulary words in context. Model conversations depict situations in which people use the words in meaningful communication. These models become the basis for students to engage in dynamic, interactive practice. In addition, writing and discussion questions in each lesson encourage students to relate the vocabulary and themes to their own lives as they share experiences, thoughts, opinions, and information about themselves, their cultures, and their countries. In this way, students get to know each other "word by word."

In using *Word by Word Basic*, we encourage you to develop approaches and strategies that are compatible with your own teaching style and the needs and abilities of your students. You may find it helpful to incorporate some of the following techniques for presenting and practicing the vocabulary in each lesson.

1. **Preview the Vocabulary:** Activate students' prior knowledge of the vocabulary by brainstorming with students the words in the lesson they already know and writing them on the board, or by having students look at the transparency or the illustration in *Word by Word Basic* and identify the words they are familiar with.

2. **Present the Vocabulary:** Using the transparency or the illustration in the Picture Dictionary, point to the picture of each word, say the word, and have the class repeat it chorally and individually. (You can also play the word list on the Audio Program.) Check students' understanding and pronunciation of the vocabulary.

3. **Vocabulary Practice:** Have students practice the vocabulary as a class, in pairs, or in small groups. Say or write a word, and have students point to the item or tell the number. Or, point to an item or give the number, and have students say the word.

4. **Model Conversation Practice:** Some lessons have model conversations that use the first word in the vocabulary list. Other models are in the form of skeletal dialogs, in which vocabulary words can be inserted. (In many skeletal dialogs, bracketed numbers indicate which words can be used for practicing the conversation. If no bracketed numbers appear, all the words in the lesson can be used.)

The following steps are recommended for Model Conversation Practice:

a. Preview: Have students look at the model illustration and discuss who they think the speakers are and where the conversation takes place.

b. The teacher presents the model or plays the audio one or more times and checks students' understanding of the situation and the vocabulary.

c. Students repeat each line of the conversation chorally and individually.

d. Students practice the model in pairs.

e. A pair of students presents a conversation based on the model, but using a different word from the vocabulary list.

f. In pairs, students practice several conversations based on the model, using different words on the page.

g. Pairs present their conversations to the class.

5. **Additional Conversation Practice:** Many lessons provide two additional skeletal dialogs for further conversation practice with the vocabulary. (These can be found in the yellow-shaded area at the bottom of the page.) Have students practice and present these conversations using any words they wish. Before they practice the additional conversations, you may want to have students listen to the sample additional conversations on the Audio Program.

6. **Spelling Practice:** Have students practice spelling the words as a class, in pairs, or in small groups. Say a word, and have students spell it aloud or write it. Or, using the transparency, point to an item and have students write the word.

7. **Themes for Discussion, Composition, Journals, and Portfolios:** Each lesson of *Word by Word Basic* provides one or more questions for discussion and composition. (These can be found in a blue-shaded area at the bottom of the page.) Have students respond to the questions as a class, in pairs, or in small groups. Or, have students write their responses at home, share their written work with other students, and discuss as a class, in pairs, or in small groups. As an alternative for students at literacy and pre-beginning levels, you can use a language experience approach by having students say their responses while you or a teaching assistant or a volunteer writes them down. Students can then practice decoding what they have "written" and then read their responses aloud to another student.

Students may enjoy keeping a journal of their written work. If time permits, you may want to write a response in each student's journal, sharing your own opinions and experiences as well as reacting to what the student has written. If you are keeping portfolios of students' work, these compositions serve as excellent examples of students' progress in learning English.

8. **Communication Activities:** The *Word by Word Basic* Teacher's Guide and Lesson Planner with CD-ROM provides a wealth of games, tasks, brainstorming, discussion, movement, drawing, miming, role-playing, and other activities designed to take advantage of students' different learning styles and particular abilities and strengths. For each lesson, choose one or more of these activities to reinforce students' vocabulary learning in a way that is stimulating, creative, and enjoyable.

WORD BY WORD BASIC aims to offer students a communicative, meaningful, and lively way of practicing English vocabulary. In conveying to you the substance of our program, we hope that we have also conveyed the spirit: that learning vocabulary can be genuinely interactive . . . relevant to our students' lives . . . responsive to students' differing strengths and learning styles . . . and fun!

Steven J. Molinsky
Bill Bliss

INFORMACIÓN PERSONAL

Gloria P. Sanchez

95 — GARDEN ST. — 3G

*Gloria P. Sanchez
95 Garden St. Apt. 3G
Los Angeles, CA 90036*

323 524-3278

323 695-1864

From: gloria97@ail.com
To:
Subject:

SOCIAL SECURITY
227-93-6185
Gloria P. Sanchez

MAY 12 1988

ENTERING CENTERVILLE POPULATION 64

Registration Form

Name	Gloria	P.	Sanchez
	First	Middle Initial	Last

Address	95	Garden Street	3G
	Number	Street	Apartment Number
	Los Angeles	CA	90036
	City	State	Zip Code

Telephone ___323-524-3278___   Cell Phone ___323-695-1864___

E-Mail Address ___gloria97@ail.com___   SSN ___227-93-6185___   Sex M__ F X

Date of Birth ___5/12/88___   Place of Birth ___Centerville, Texas___

nombre completo	**1** name	código/zona postal	**11** zip code
nombre de pila	**2** first name	código/prefijo telefónico/ clave telefónica	**12** area code
inicial del segundo nombre	**3** middle initial	número de teléfono	**13** telephone number/ phone number
apellidos (paterno y materno)	**4** last name/ family name	número de teléfono celular/móvil	**14** cell phone number
domicilio	**5** address	dirección de correo electrónico	**15** e-mail address
número de la casa	**6** street number	número de seguro social	**16** social security number
calle	**7** street	sexo	**17** sex
número del apartamento	**8** apartment number	fecha de nacimiento	**18** date of birth
ciudad	**9** city	lugar de nacimiento	**19** place of birth
estado/provincia/ departamento	**10** state		

A. What's your **name**?
B. Gloria P. Sanchez.

A. What's your _____?
B. ....
A. Did you say ....?
B. Yes. That's right.

A. What's your last name?
B. ....
A. How do you spell that?
B. ....

Tell about yourself:
    My name is ....
    My address is ....
    My telephone number is ....

Now interview a friend:
    What's your name?
    What's your address?
    What's your telephone number?

LA FAMILIA (INMEDIATA) I

esposo	**1** husband		hermanos(as)	**siblings**
esposa	**2** wife		hermana	**8** sister
			hermano	**9** brother
padres	**parents**			
padre/papá	**3** father		**abuelos**	**grandparents**
madre/mamá	**4** mother		abuela	**10** grandmother
			abuelo	**11** grandfather
hijos	**children**			
hija	**5** daughter		**nietos**	**grandchildren**
hijo	**6** son		nieta	**12** granddaughter
bebé/nene(a)	**7** baby		nieto	**13** grandson

A. Who is he?
B. He's my **husband**.
A. What's his name?
B. His name is *Jack*.

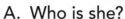

A. Who is she?
B. She's my **wife**.
A. What's her name?
B. Her name is *Nancy*.

A. I'd like to introduce my _____.
B. Nice to meet you.
C. Nice to meet you, too.

A. What's your _____'s name?
B. His/Her name is ....

Who are the people in your family?
What are their names?

Tell about photos of family members.

FAMILY MEMBERS II

LA FAMILIA (PARIENTES) II

Helen

Walter

Jack

Nancy

Frank

Linda

Jennifer

Timmy

Alan

tío	**1** uncle	primo/prima	**5** cousin	yerno	**8** son-in-law
tía	**2** aunt	suegra	**6** mother-in-law	nuera	**9** daughter-in-law
sobrina	**3** niece	suegro	**7** father-in-law	cuñado	**10** brother-in-law
sobrino	**4** nephew			cuñada	**11** sister-in-law

(1) Jack is Alan's ___.

(2) Nancy is Alan's ___.

(3) Jennifer is Frank and Linda's ___.

(4) Timmy is Frank and Linda's ___.

(5) Alan is Jennifer and Timmy's ___.

(6) Helen is Jack's ___.

(7) Walter is Jack's ___.

(8) Jack is Helen and Walter's ___.

(9) Linda is Helen and Walter's ___.

(10) Frank is Jack's ___.

(11) Linda is Jack's ___.

A. Who is he/she?

B. He's/She's my _____.

A. What's his/her name?

B. His/Her name is _____.

A. Let me introduce my _____.

B. I'm glad to meet you.

C. Nice meeting you, too.

Tell about your relatives:
   What are their names?
   Where do they live?

Draw your family tree and tell about it.

CLASSROOM OBJECTS

OBJETOS DEL SALÓN/LA SALA DE CLASES/EL AULA

bolígrafo/pluma (estilográfica)/lapicero	**1** pen	papel cuadriculado	**10** graph paper
lápiz/lapicero	**2** pencil	regla	**11** ruler
borrador/goma de borrar	**3** eraser	calculadora	**12** calculator
sacapuntas	**4** pencil sharpener	tiza/gis/pizarrín	**13** chalk
libro/texto	**5** book/textbook	borrador	**14** eraser
cuaderno/manual de ejercicios/de actividades	**6** workbook	marcador	**15** marker
		tachuela/chinche/chincheta	**16** thumbtack
cuaderno/carpeta con espiral	**7** spiral notebook	teclado	**17** keyboard
carpeta/portafolios	**8** binder/notebook	pantalla/monitor	**18** monitor
papel para carpetas/ para portafolios	**9** notebook paper	ratón	**19** mouse
		impresora	**20** printer

[1, 2, 4–13, 15–20]

A. What do you call this in English?
B. It's a **pen**.

[3, 14]

A. What do you call this in English?
B. It's an **eraser**.

A. Where's the _____?
B. Over there.

[1–3, 5–12]
A. Is this your _____?
B. Yes, it is.

Point to objects and people in your classroom and say the words.

THE CLASSROOM

EL SALÓN/LA SALA DE CLASES/EL AULA

maestro(a)	**1** teacher		mapa	**12** map
asistente/auxiliar	**2** teacher's aide		cartelera/tablero/tablilla/ mural/de anuncios	**13** bulletin board
alumno(a)/estudiante	**3** student		sistema de altavoz/ altoparlante	**14** P.A. system / loudspeaker
pupitre/escritorio	**4** desk		pizarra /pizarrón/ tablero para marcadores	**15** whiteboard
silla/banco	**5** seat / chair		globo terráqueo/del mundo	**16** globe
mesa	**6** table		librera/librero/librería/ estante para libros	**17** bookcase / bookshelf
computadora/ordenador	**7** computer		escritorio de la maestra/ del maestro	**18** teacher's desk
retroproyector/proyector de transparencias	**8** overhead projector		papelera/cesto/canasta de papeles	**19** wastebasket
pantalla	**9** screen			
pizarra/pizarrón/ tablero	**10** board / chalkboard			
reloj	**11** clock			

Practice these conversations with the words on pages 8–11.

A. Where's the **teacher**?
B. The **teacher** is *next to* the **board**.

A. Where's the **globe**?
B. The **globe** is *on* the **bookcase**.

A. Is there a/an ____ in your classroom?*
B. Yes. There's a/an ____ next to/on the ____.

A. Is there a/an ____ in your classroom?*
B. No, there isn't.

Describe your classroom. (There's a/an ....)

* With 9, 10, 13 on page 9, use: Is there ____ in your classroom?

ACCIONES EN EL SALÓN/LA SALA DE CLASES/EL AULA I

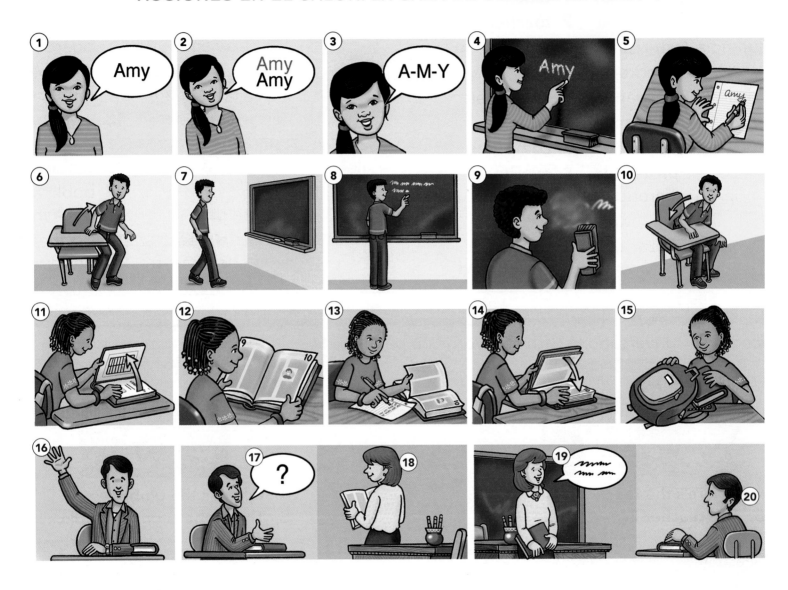

Diga(n) su nombre.	1	Say your name.
Repita(n) su nombre.	2	Repeat your name.
Deletree(n) su nombre.	3	Spell your name.
Escriba(n) su nombre.	4	Print your name.
Firme(n).	5	Sign your name.

Abra(n) el libro.	11	Open your book.
Lea(n) la página diez.	12	Read page ten.
Estudie(n) la página diez.	13	Study page ten.
Cierre(n) el libro.	14	Close your book.
Guarde(n) el libro.	15	Put away your book.

Levánte(n)se.	6	Stand up.
Vaya(n) a la pizarra/al pizarrón/tablero.	7	Go to the board.
Escriba(n) en la pizarra/el pizarrón/tablero.	8	Write on the board.
Borre(n) la pizarra/el pizarrón/tablero.	9	Erase the board.
Siénte(n)se/Tome(n) asiento.	10	Sit down. / Take your seat.

Levante(n)/Alce(n) la mano.	16	Raise your hand.
Haga(n) una pregunta./Pregunte(n).	17	Ask a question.
Escuche(n) la pregunta.	18	Listen to the question.
Conteste(n) la pregunta.	19	Answer the question.
Escuche(n) la respuesta.	20	Listen to the answer.

You're the teacher.
Give instructions to your students.

CLASSROOM ACTIONS II

ACCIONES EN EL SALÓN/LA SALA DE CLASES/EL AULA II

Spanish	#	English
Haga(n) su tarea/ sus deberes.	1	Do your homework.
Traiga(n) su tarea/ sus deberes.	2	Bring in your homework.
Revise(n) las respuestas/ las contestaciones.	3	Go over the answers.
Corrija(n) sus errores.	4	Correct your mistakes.
Entregue(n) su tarea.	5	Hand in your homework.

Spanish	#	English
Consulte(n) el diccionario.	11	Look in the dictionary.
Busque(n) una palabra.	12	Look up a word.
Pronuncie(n) la palabra.	13	Pronounce the word.
Lea(n) la definición.	14	Read the definition.
Copie(n) la palabra.	15	Copy the word.

Spanish	#	English
Comparta(n) un libro.	6	Share a book.
Discuta(n) la pregunta.	7	Discuss the question.
Ayúdense.	8	Help each other.
Trabajen juntos(as).	9	Work together.
Comparta(n) con la clase.	10	Share with the class.

Spanish	#	English
Trabaje(n) individualmente.	16	Work alone./ Do your own work.
Trabajen en parejas/ pares.	17	Work with a partner.
Divídanse en equipos/ grupos pequeños.	18	Break up into small groups.
Trabaje(n) en grupos/ equipos.	19	Work in a group.
Trabaje(n) con toda la clase.	20	Work as a class.

You're the teacher.
Give instructions to your students.

ACCIONES EN EL SALÓN/LA SALA DE CLASES/EL AULA III

Baje(n) las persianas.	**1** Lower the shades.
Apague(n) las luces.	**2** Turn off the lights.
Mire(n) la pantalla.	**3** Look at the screen.
Tome(n) notas.	**4** Take notes.
Prenda(n)/Ponga(n)/ Encienda(n) las luces.	**5** Turn on the lights.

Escoja(n)/Elija(n) la respuesta correcta.	**11** Choose the correct answer.
Encierre(n) en un círculo la respuesta correcta.	**12** Circle the correct answer.
Llene(n) el espacio.	**13** Fill in the blank.
Rellene(n) el círculo.	**14** Mark the answer sheet. / Bubble the answer.
Relacione(n)/Paree(n) las palabras.	**15** Match the words.

Saque(n) un papel.	**6** Take out a piece of paper.
Pase(n) los exámenes/las pruebas.	**7** Pass out the tests.
Conteste(n) las preguntas.	**8** Answer the questions.
Revise(n) sus respuestas/ sus contestaciones.	**9** Check your answers.
Entregue(n) los exámenes/las pruebas.	**10** Collect the tests.

Subraye(n) la palabra.	**16** Underline the word.
Tache(n) la palabra.	**17** Cross out the word.
Ordene(n)/acomode(n) las letras de la palabra.	**18** Unscramble the word.
Ordene(n)/Acomode(n) las palabras.	**19** Put the words in order.
Escriba(n) en una hoja aparte.	**20** Write on a separate sheet of paper.

You're the teacher.
Give instructions to your students.

PREPOSICIONES

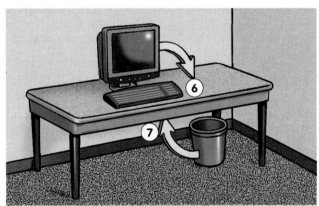

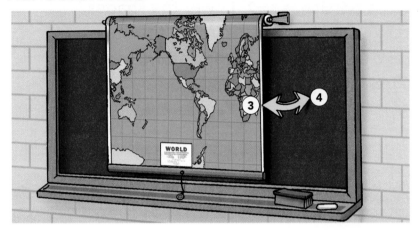

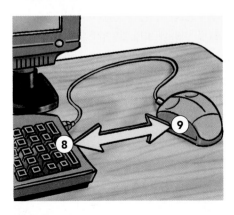

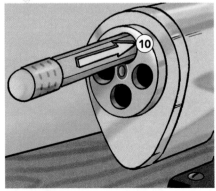

arriba **1** above

abajo **2** below

enfrente/delante (de) **3** in front of

detrás (de) **4** behind

junto a **5** next to

sobre **6** on

bajo/debajo (de) **7** under

a la izquierda de **8** to the left of

a la derecha de **9** to the right of

en/dentro (de) **10** in

entre **11** between

[1–10]

A. Where's the *clock*?

B. The *clock* is **above** the *bulletin board*.

[11]

A. Where's the *dictionary*?

B. The *dictionary* is **between** the *globe* and the *pencil sharpener*.

Tell about the classroom on page 10. Use the prepositions in this lesson.

Tell about your classroom.

PEOPLE AND PLACES AT SCHOOL

PERSONAS E LUGARES EN LA ESCUELA

oficina/administración	**A** office	secretario(a) de la escuela	**1** clerk / (school) secretary
dirección/rectoría	**B** principal's office	director(a)	**2** principal
enfermería	**C** nurse's office	enfermero(a)	**3** school nurse
consejería	**D** guidance office	consejero(a)	**4** guidance counselor
salón/sala de clases/aula	**E** classroom	maestro(a)/profesor(a)	**5** teacher
pasillo/corredor	**F** hallway	subdirector(a)	**6** assistant principal / vice-principal
casillero	**a** locker		
laboratorio de ciencias	**G** science lab	guardia de seguridad	**7** security officer
gimnasio	**H** gym	maestro(a) de ciencias	**8** science teacher
vestidor	**a** locker room	maestro(a) de educación física	**9** P.E. teacher
pista	**I** track		
gradería/gradas	**a** bleachers	entrenador(a)	**10** coach
campo de juego	**J** field	portero(a)/afanador(a)	**11** custodian
auditorio	**K** auditorium	empleado(a) de la cafetería	**12** cafeteria worker
cafetería	**L** cafeteria	supervisor(a) de la cafetería	**13** lunchroom monitor
biblioteca	**M** library	bibliotecario(a)	**14** school librarian

A. Where are you going?
B. I'm going to the ___[A–D, G–M]___ .
A. Do you have a hall pass?
B. Yes. Here it is.

A. Where's the ___[1–14]___ ?
B. He's⎫
   She's⎭ in the ___[A–M]___ .

Describe the school where you study English.
Tell about the rooms, offices, and people.

Tell about differences between the school in this lesson and schools in your country.

EVERYDAY ACTIVITIES I

HÁBITOS Y QUEHACERES DOMÉSTICOS I

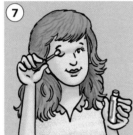

me levanto	**1**	get up	*me* desvisto	**11** get undressed
me baño/*me* ducho	**2**	take a shower	*me* baño/*me* meto en la tina	**12** take a bath
me lavo/*me* cepillo los dientes	**3**	brush *my** teeth	*me* acuesto	**13** go to bed
me afeito/*me* rasuro	**4**	shave	*me* duermo	**14** sleep
me visto	**5**	get dressed	hago/preparo el desayuno	**15** make breakfast
me lavo la cara	**6**	wash *my** face	hago/preparo el almuerzo	**16** make lunch
me maquillo/*me* pinto	**7**	put on makeup	hago/preparo la cena	**17** cook/make dinner
me cepillo el pelo/cabello	**8**	brush *my** hair	desayuno	**18** eat/have breakfast
me peino el pelo/cabello	**9**	comb *my** hair	almuerzo	**19** eat/have lunch
hago/tiendo la cama	**10**	make the bed	ceno	**20** eat/have dinner

* my, his, her, our, your, their

A. What do you do every day?
B. I **get up**, I **take a shower**, and I **brush my teeth**.

A. What does he do every day?
B. He _____s, he _____s, and he _____s.

A. What does she do every day?
B. She _____s, she _____s, and she_____s.

What do you do every day? Make a list.

Interview some friends and tell about their everyday activities.

EVERYDAY ACTIVITIES II

HÁBITOS Y QUEHACERES DOMÉSTICOS II

limpiar el apartamento/ departamento/la casa	**1** clean the apartment/ clean the house	ir al trabajo	**9** go to work
lavar los platos/trastos	**2** wash the dishes	ir a la escuela/al colegio	**10** go to school
lavar la ropa	**3** do the laundry	manejar/conducir al trabajo	**11** drive to work
alisar con la plancha/ planchar	**4** iron	tomar el autobús/bus/ camión para ir a la escuela	**12** take the bus to school
darle de comer al bebé/ a la bebé/al nene/ a la nena	**5** feed the baby	trabajar	**13** work
		salir del trabajo	**14** leave work
darle de comer al gato	**6** feed the cat	ir a la tienda	**15** go to the store
pasear al perro	**7** walk the dog	llegar a casa	**16** come home
estudiar	**8** study		

A. Hello. What are you doing?
B. I'm **clean**ing the **apartment**.

A. Hello, ... This is ....
What are you doing?
B. I'm _____ing. How about you?
A. I'm _____ing.

A. Are you going to _____ soon?
B. Yes. I'm going to _____ in a little while.

What are you going to do tomorrow? Make a list of everything you are going to do.

LEISURE ACTIVITIES

ACTIVIDADES RECREATIVAS

ver la televisión/tele	**1**	watch TV	tocar la guitarra	**9** play the guitar
oír/escuchar el/la radio	**2**	listen to the radio	tocar el piano	**10** practice the piano
oír/escuchar música	**3**	listen to music	hacer ejercicio	**11** exercise
leer un libro	**4**	read a book	nadar	**12** swim
leer el periódico/ diario	**5**	read the newspaper	sembrar/plantar flores	**13** plant flowers
jugar	**6**	play	usar la computadora/ el ordenador	**14** use the computer
jugar barajas/a los naipes/ las cartas	**7**	play cards	escribir una carta	**15** write a letter
jugar baloncesto/ básquetbol	**8**	play basketball	descansar/relajarse	**16** relax

A. Hi. What are you doing?
B. I'm **watch**ing **TV**.

A. Hi, ... Are you
   _____ing?
B. No, I'm not. I'm _____ing.

A. What's your (husband/wife/son/ daughter/. . .) doing?
B. He's/She's _____ing.

What leisure activities do you like to do?

What do your family members and friends like to do?

EVERYDAY CONVERSATION I

CONVERSACIONES DIARIAS I

Greeting People

Saludos

Leave Taking

Despididas

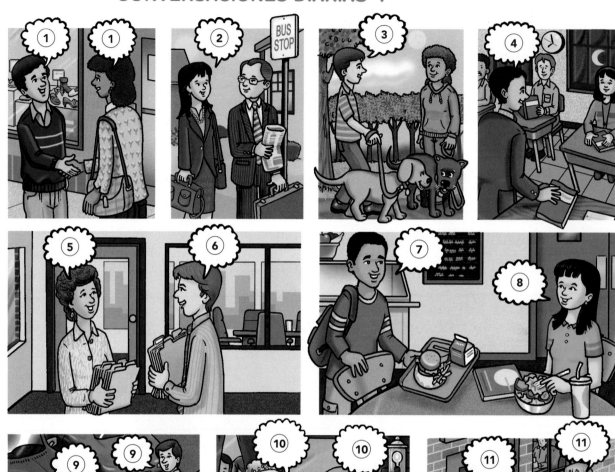

Hola.	**1**	Hello. / Hi.
Buenos días.	**2**	Good morning.
Buenas tardes.	**3**	Good afternoon.
Buenas noches./Buenas tardes.	**4**	Good evening.
¿Cómo está(s)?/¿Cómo le va?/¿Cómo te va?	**5**	How are you?/How are you doing?
Bien./Bien, gracias.	**6**	Fine./Fine, thanks./Okay.
¿Qué hay de nuevo?/¿Qué te cuentas?	**7**	What's new?/What's new with you?
Nada./No mucho.	**8**	Not much./Not too much.
Adiós.	**9**	Good-bye./Bye.
Buenas noches.	**10**	Good night.
Hasta luego./Hasta pronto.	**11**	See you later./See you soon.

Practice conversations with other students.
Use all the expressions in this lesson.

CONVERSACIONES DIARIAS II

Introducing Yourself and Others
Presentaciones

Getting Someone's Attention
Expresiones para llamar la atención

Expressing Gratitude
Expresiones de agradecimiento

Saying You Don't Understand
Expresiones de duda

Calling Someone on the Telephone
En el teléfono

Hola. Me llamo	**1**	Hello. My name is .... / Hi. I'm ....
Mucho gusto.	**2**	Nice to meet you.
El gusto es mío.	**3**	Nice to meet you, too.
Le/Te presento a	**4**	I'd like to introduce .... / This is ....
Permiso./Disculpe(a).	**5**	Excuse me.
¿Puedo hacerle(te) una pregunta?	**6**	May I ask a question?
Gracias.	**7**	Thank you. / Thanks.
De nada./No hay de qué.	**8**	You're welcome.
¿Cómo?/No entiendo./Disculpe(a). No entiendo.	**9**	I don't understand. / Sorry. I don't understand.
¿Repita(e), por favor?	**10**	Can you please repeat that?/ Can you please say that again?
Hola. Habla .... ¿Podría/ Puedo hablar con ....?/¿Está ....?	**11**	Hello. This is .... May I please speak to ....?
Sí, un momento, por favor.	**12**	Yes. Hold on a moment.
Lo siento, ... no está aquí en este momento./Lo siento, ... no se encuentra en este momento.	**13**	I'm sorry. .... isn't here right now.

Practice conversations with other students.
Use all the expressions in this lesson.

EL ESTADO DEL TIEMPO

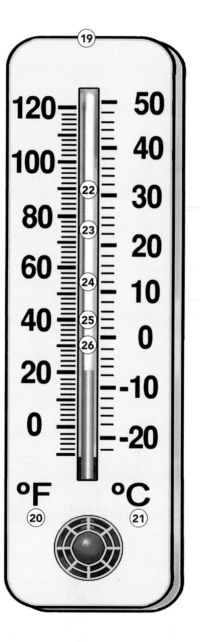

El estado del tiempo	Weather		relámpagos/truenos/rayos	14	lightning
está soleado	**1** sunny		tormenta de rayos/de truenos	**15**	thunderstorm
está nublado/nuboso	**2** cloudy		tormenta de nieve	**16**	snowstorm
está despejado/claro	**3** clear		tolvanera/polvareda	**17**	dust storm
hay bruma/calina	**4** hazy		ola de calor	**18**	heat wave
hay niebla/neblina	**5** foggy				
está contaminado	**6** smoggy		**La temperatura**	**Temperature**	
hace viento/está ventoso/sopla viento	**7** windy		termómetro	**19**	thermometer
			Fahrenheit	**20**	Fahrenheit
está húmedo/pegajoso/ bochornoso	**8** humid / muggy		Centígrados/ Celsius	**21**	Centigrade/ Celsius
llueve	**9** raining		hace calor	**22**	hot
llovizna	**10** drizzling		es (un día/un clima) caluroso/cálido	**23**	warm
cae nieve/nieva	**11** snowing		hace fresco	**24**	cool
graniza	**12** hailing		hace frío	**25**	cold
cellisquea/cae aguanieve/ una helada	**13** sleeting		está helado	**26**	freezing

[1–13]

A. What's the weather like?

B. It's _____.

[14–18]

A. What's the weather forecast?

B. There's going to be ⎰ ___[14]___ .
⎱ a ___[15–18]___ .

[20–26]

A. How's the weather?

B. It's ___[22–26]___ .

A. What's the temperature?

B. It's . . . degrees ___[20–21]___ .

What's the weather like today? What's the temperature?   What's the weather forecast for tomorrow?

CARDINAL NUMBERS

LOS NÚMEROS CARDINALES

0 zero	**11** eleven	**21** twenty-one	**101** one hundred (and) one
1 one	**12** twelve	**22** twenty-two	**102** one hundred (and) two
2 two	**13** thirteen	**30** thirty	**1,000** one thousand
3 three	**14** fourteen	**40** forty	**10,000** ten thousand
4 four	**15** fifteen	**50** fifty	**100,000** one hundred thousand
5 five	**16** sixteen	**60** sixty	**1,000,000** one million
6 six	**17** seventeen	**70** seventy	**1,000,000,000** one billion
7 seven	**18** eighteen	**80** eighty	
8 eight	**19** nineteen	**90** ninety	
9 nine	**20** twenty	**100** one hundred	
10 ten			

A. How old are you?
B. I'm _____ years old.

A. How many people are there in your family?
B. _____.

How many students are there in your class?

How many people are there in your country?

LOS NÚMEROS ORDINALES

1st	first	**11th**	eleventh	**21st**	twenty-first	**101st**	one hundred (and) first
2nd	second	**12th**	twelfth	**22nd**	twenty-second	**102nd**	one hundred (and) second
3rd	third	**13th**	thirteenth	**30th**	thirtieth	**1,000th**	one thousandth
4th	fourth	**14th**	fourteenth	**40th**	fortieth	**10,000th**	ten thousandth
5th	fifth	**15th**	fifteenth	**50th**	fiftieth	**100,000th**	one hundred thousandth
6th	sixth	**16th**	sixteenth	**60th**	sixtieth	**1,000,000th**	one millionth
7th	seventh	**17th**	seventeenth	**70th**	seventieth	**1,000,000,000th**	one billionth
8th	eighth	**18th**	eighteenth	**80th**	eightieth		
9th	ninth	**19th**	nineteenth	**90th**	ninetieth		
10th	tenth	**20th**	twentieth	**100th**	one hundredth		

A. What floor do you live on?
B. I live on the _____ floor.

A. Is this your first trip to our country?
B. No. It's my _____ trip.

What were the names of your teachers in elementary school?
(My *first*-grade teacher was Ms./Mrs./Mr. . . .)

LA HORA

two o'clock

two fifteen/
a quarter after two

two thirty/
half past two

two forty-five/
a quarter to three

two oh five

two twenty/
twenty after two

two forty/
twenty to three

two fifty-five/
five to three

A. What time is it?
B. It's _____.

A. What time does the movie begin?
B. At _____.

two A.M.

two P.M.

noon /
twelve noon

midnight /
twelve midnight

A. When does the train leave?
B. At _____.

A. What time will we arrive?
B. At _____.

Tell about your daily schedule:
    What do you do? When?
    (I get up at _____. I ....)

Tell about the use of time in different cultures or countries you know:
    Do people arrive on time for work? appointments? parties?
    Do trains and buses operate exactly on schedule?
    Do movies and sports events begin on time?
    Do workplaces use time clocks or timesheets to record employees' work hours?

MONEDA SUELTA/SUELTO/SENCILLO

	Name	Value	Written as:	
1	penny	one cent	1¢	$ .01
2	nickel	five cents	5¢	$ .05
3	dime	ten cents	10¢	$ .10
4	quarter	twenty-five cents	25¢	$ .25
5	half dollar	fifty cents	50¢	$ .50
6	silver dollar	one dollar		$1.00

A. How much is a **penny** worth?

B. A **penny** is worth **one cent**.

A. *Soda* costs *ninety-five cents.*
   Do you have enough change?

B. Yes. I have a/two/three ____(s) and . . . .

PAPEL MONEDA

Name	We sometimes say:	Value	Written as:
1 (one-) dollar bill	a one	one dollar	$ 1.00
2 five-dollar bill	a five	five dollars	$ 5.00
3 ten-dollar bill	a ten	ten dollars	$ 10.00
4 twenty-dollar bill	a twenty	twenty dollars	$ 20.00
5 fifty-dollar bill	a fifty	fifty dollars	$ 50.00
6 (one-) hundred dollar bill	a hundred	one hundred dollars	$ 100.00

A. Do you have any cash?
B. Yes. I have a **twenty-dollar bill**.

A. Can you change a **five-dollar bill**?
B. Yes. I have *five* **one-dollar bills**.

Written as:	We say:
$1.30	a dollar and thirty cents a dollar thirty
$2.50	two dollars and fifty cents two fifty
$56.49	fifty-six dollars and forty-nine cents fifty-six forty-nine

Tell about some things you usually buy.
What do they cost?

Name and describe the coins and currency in your country.
What are they worth in U.S. dollars?

EL CALENDARIO

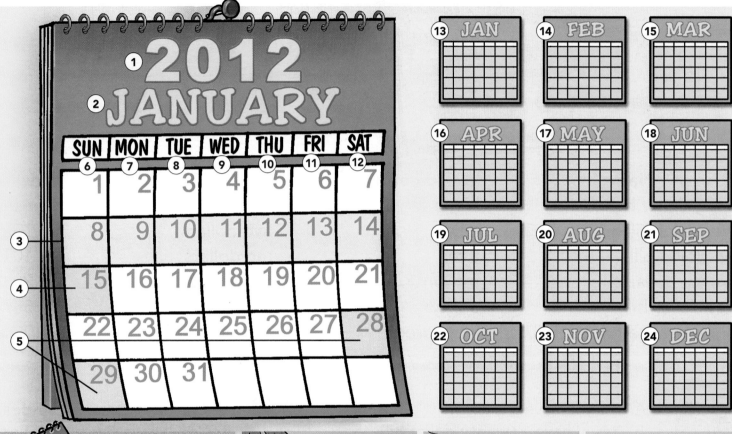

2012 ①
JANUARY ②

⑥ SUN	⑦ MON	⑧ TUE	⑨ WED	⑩ THU	⑪ FRI	⑫ SAT
1	2	3	4	5	6	7
8	9	10	11	12	13	14
15	16	17	18	19	20	21
22	23	24	25	26	27	28
29	30	31				

③ ④ ⑤

⑬ JAN   ⑭ FEB   ⑮ MAR

⑯ APR   ⑰ MAY   ⑱ JUN

⑲ JUL   ⑳ AUG   ㉑ SEP

㉒ OCT   ㉓ NOV   ㉔ DEC

2012 JANUARY

㉕ **1/3/12**

JAN 3 2012

㉖

HAPPY 25th

㉗

㉘ APPOINTMENT
Charles Wong, M.D.
Date: *February 21*
Time: *3:00 PM*

año	**1** year
mes	**2** month
semana	**3** week
día	**4** day
fin de semana	**5** weekend

Los días de la semana — **Days of the Week**

domingo	**6** Sunday
lunes	**7** Monday
martes	**8** Tuesday
miércoles	**9** Wednesday
jueves	**10** Thursday
viernes	**11** Friday
sábado	**12** Saturday

Los meses del año — **Months of the Year**

enero	**13** January
febrero	**14** February
marzo	**15** March
abril	**16** April
mayo	**17** May
junio	**18** June
julio	**19** July
agosto	**20** August
septiembre	**21** September
octubre	**22** October
noviembre	**23** November
diciembre	**24** December

3 de enero de 2012 el tres de enero de dos mil doce	**25** January 3, 2012 January third, two thousand twelve
cumpleaños	**26** birthday
aniversario	**27** anniversary
cita	**28** appointment

A. What year is it?
B. It's _____.

[13–24]
A. What month is it?
B. It's _____.

[6–12]
A. What day is it?
B. It's _____.

A. What's today's date?
B. It's _____.

[26–28]
A. When is your _____?
B. It's on _____.

Which days of the week do you go to work/school?
(I go to work/school on _____.)

What is your date of birth?
(I was born on ..._month day, year_...)

What's your favorite day of the week? Why?

What's your favorite month of the year? Why?

EXPRESIONES DE TIEMPO Y LAS ESTACIONES

ayer	**1**	yesterday		
hoy	**2**	today		
mañana	**3**	tomorrow		
por la mañana	**4**	morning		
por la tarde	**5**	afternoon		
por la tardecita/nochecita/ al atardecer/anochecer	**6**	evening		
por la noche	**7**	night		
ayer por la mañana	**8**	yesterday morning		
ayer por la tarde	**9**	yesterday afternoon		
ayer por la tardecita/ nochecita/al atardecer/ anochecer	**10**	yesterday evening		
anoche	**11**	last night		
esta mañana	**12**	this morning		
esta tarde	**13**	this afternoon		
por la tardecita/nochecita/ al atardecer/al anochecer	**14**	this evening		
esta noche	**15**	tonight		

mañana por la mañana	**16**	tomorrow morning
mañana por la tarde	**17**	tomorrow afternoon
mañana por la tardecita/ nochecita/al atardecer/ anochecer	**18**	tomorrow evening
mañana por la noche	**19**	tomorrow night
la semana pasada	**20**	last week
esta semana	**21**	this week
la próxima semana/ la semana entrante	**22**	next week
una vez a la semana	**23**	once a week
dos veces a la semana	**24**	twice a week
tres veces a la semana	**25**	three times a week
todos los días/a diario	**26**	every day

Las estaciones Seasons

primavera	**27**	spring
verano	**28**	summer
otoño	**29**	fall/autumn
invierno	**30**	winter

What did you do yesterday morning/afternoon/ evening?

What did you do last night?

What are you going to do tomorrow morning/ afternoon/evening/night?

What did you do last week?

What are your plans for next week?

How many times a week do you have English class?/go to the supermarket?/exercise?

What's your favorite season? Why?

TYPES OF HOUSING AND COMMUNITIES

TIPOS DE VIVIENDA Y COMUNIDADES

edificio de apartamentos/departamentos	**1**	apartment building
casa	**2**	house
dúplex	**3**	duplex/two-family house
casas (de 2 ó 3 plantas) en hileras	**4**	townhouse/townhome
condominio/condo/piso	**5**	condominium/condo
dormitorio/residencia estudiantil	**6**	dormitory/dorm
casa prefabricada/móvil/rodante	**7**	mobile home
asilo/casa de ancianos/de reposo	**8**	nursing home
refugio/asilo para desvalidos/albergue para desamparados	**9**	shelter
hacienda/granja/finca	**10**	farm
rancho	**11**	ranch
casa flotante	**12**	houseboat
la ciudad	**13**	the city
los suburbios/las afueras	**14**	the suburbs
el campo	**15**	the country
un pueblo/un poblado/una villa	**16**	a town/village

A. Where do you live?

B. I live
- in a/an ___[1–9]___.
- on a ___[10–12]___.
- in ___[13–16]___.

[1–12]

A. Town Taxi Company.
B. Hello. Please send a taxi to .....(address).....
A. Is that a house or an apartment building?
B. It's a/an _____.
A. All right. We'll be there right away.

[1–12]

A. This is the Emergency Operator.
B. Please send an ambulance to .....(address).....
A. Is that a private home?
B. It's a/an _____.
A. What's your name and telephone number?
B. ....

Tell about people you know and where they live.

Discuss:
Who lives in dormitories?
Who lives in nursing homes?
Who lives in shelters?
Why?

THE LIVING ROOM

LA SALA

librero/librería/ estante para libros	**1** bookcase	mueble/unidad de pared	**15** wall unit
foto/fotografía/retrato	**2** picture/ photograph	bocina/altoparlante/altavoz	**16** speaker
		estéreo/equipo estereofónico	**17** stereo system
cuadro/pintura	**3** painting	revistero	**18** magazine holder
manto de la chimenea/del hogar	**4** mantel		
hogar/chimenea	**5** fireplace	cojín	**19** pillow
pantalla/rejilla de la chimenea	**6** fireplace screen	sofá	**20** sofa/couch
DVD/reproductor de video digital	**7** DVD player	mata/planta	**21** plant
televisor/TV/televisión/tele	**8** television/TV	mesa de centro	**22** coffee table
videocasetera/videograbadora	**9** VCR/video cassette recorder	alfombra/alfombrilla/tapete	**23** rug
		lámpara	**24** lamp
pared/muro/tapia	**10** wall	pantalla	**25** lampshade
cielo raso/techo	**11** ceiling	mesita/esquinera/mesilla	**26** end table
cortinas	**12** drapes	piso	**27** floor
ventana	**13** window	lámpara de pie	**28** floor lamp
confidente/canapé/sofá	**14** loveseat	sillón/silla de brazos/butaca	**29** armchair

A. Where are you?
B. I'm in the living room.
A. What are you doing?
B. I'm dusting* the **bookcase**.

*dusting/cleaning

A. You have a very nice living room!
B. Thank you.
A. Your _____ is/are beautiful!
B. Thank you for saying so.

A. Uh-oh! I just spilled coffee on your _____!
B. That's okay. Don't worry about it.

Tell about your living room.
(In my living room there's ....)

EL COMEDOR

mesa de comedor	**1**	(dining room) table	candela/vela	**17**	candle
silla de comedor	**2**	(dining room) chair	candelero	**18**	candlestick
aparador	**3**	buffet	bandeja	**19**	platter
bandeja/charola	**4**	tray	mantequillera	**20**	butter dish
tetera	**5**	teapot	salero	**21**	salt shaker
cafetera	**6**	coffee pot	pimentero	**22**	pepper shaker
azucarera	**7**	sugar bowl	mantel	**23**	tablecloth
jarrita para la leche/crema	**8**	creamer	servilleta	**24**	napkin
jarro(a)	**9**	pitcher	tenedor/trinche	**25**	fork
lámpara de araña/de techo/	**10**	chandelier	plato	**26**	plate
candil de techo			cuchillo	**27**	knife
armario/alacena/vitrina/chinero	**11**	china cabinet	cuchara	**28**	spoon
vajilla/vajilla de porcelana/loza	**12**	china	plato hondo/tazón	**29**	bowl
ensaladera	**13**	salad bowl	taza	**30**	mug
sopera/fuente honda	**14**	serving bowl	vaso	**31**	glass
bandeja	**15**	serving dish	taza	**32**	cup
florero/jarrón	**16**	vase	plato pequeño/platito/platillo	**33**	saucer

A. This **dining room table** is very nice.
B. Thank you. It was a gift from my *grandmother*.*

*grandmother/grandfather/aunt/uncle/. . .

[In a store]
A. May I help you?
B. Yes, please. Do you have _____s?*
A. Yes. _____s* are right over there.
B. Thank you.

*With 12, use the singular.

[At home]
A. Where did you get this old _____?
B. At a yard sale. How do you like it?
A. It's VERY unusual!

Tell about your dining room.
(In my dining room there's
.............)

THE BEDROOM

LA RECÁMARA/EL DORMITORIO

cama	**1** bed		cortinas	**13** curtains
cabecera	**2** headboard		lámpara	**14** lamp
almohada	**3** pillow		despertador	**15** alarm clock
funda	**4** pillowcase		radio reloj despertador	**16** clock radio
sábana	**5** sheet		mesita/mesa de noche/	**17** night table/
manta/frazada/cobija/frisa	**6** blanket		buró	nightstand
manta/cobija/frisa eléctrica	**7** electric blanket		espejo	**18** mirror
colcha/cubrecama/	**8** bedspread		joyero/alhajero	**19** jewelry box
sobrecama			cómoda/tocador	**20** dresser/bureau
edredón/cobertor relleno	**9** comforter/quilt		colchón	**21** mattress
alfombra	**10** carpet		colchón de muelles	**22** box spring
chifonier/ropero/gavetero	**11** chest (of drawers)		marco/armadura	**23** bed frame
persianas	**12** blinds			

A. Ooh! Look at that big bug!
B. Where?
A. It's on the **bed**!
B. I'LL get it.

[In a store]

A. Excuse me. I'm looking for
a/an _____.*
B. We have some very nice _____s,
and they're all on sale this week!
A. Oh, good!

* With 12 & 13, use: Excuse me. I'm looking for ____.

[In a bedroom]

A. Oh, no! I just lost my
contact lens!
B. Where?
A. I think it's on the _____.
B. I'll help you look.

Tell about your bedroom.
(In my bedroom there's ....)

THE KITCHEN

LA COCINA

refrigerador(a)/nevera	**1** refrigerator	lavaplatos/lavavajillas	**13** dishwasher	tacho/hervidor	**23** tea kettle	
congelador	**2** freezer	triturador de desperdicios	**14** (garbage) disposal	estufa/cocina	**24** stove/range	
cubo/bote de basura/basurero/tinaco/zafacón	**3** garbage pail	trapo/paño/toalla de cocina/limpión	**15** dish towel	horno	**25** oven	
batidora eléctrica/mezcladora eléctrica	**4** (electric) mixer	escurridor de platos	**16** dish rack	tostador/tostadora	**26** toaster	
estante/armario/gabinete	**5** cabinet	especiero/repisa para especias/condimentos	**17** spice rack	cafetera	**27** coffeemaker	
colgador para papel toalla	**6** paper towel holder			compresor de basura	**28** trash compactor	
envases/tarrones/recipientes para harina, azúcar, té o sal	**7** canister	abrelatas eléctrico	**18** (electric) can opener	tablita/tabla para picar/picador	**29** cutting board	
mostrador	**8** counter	licuadora eléctrica	**19** blender	libro de recetas de cocina	**30** cookbook	
jabón para el lavaplatos/lavavajillas	**9** dishwasher detergent	hornito/horno pastelero/tostador	**20** toaster oven	molinillo/procesador de alimentos	**31** food processor	
líquido de fregar/lavar los platos	**10** dishwashing liquid	horno microondas	**21** microwave	silla	**32** kitchen chair	
grifo/llave/pluma	**11** faucet	agarrador de ollas	**22** potholder	mesa	**33** kitchen table	
fregadero/fregador	**12** sink			individual/mantelito individual	**34** placemat	

A. I think we need a new **refrigerator**.
B. I think you're right.

[In a store]
A. Excuse me. Are your _____s still on sale?
B. Yes, they are. They're twenty percent off.

[In a kitchen]
A. When did you get this/these new _____(s)?
B. I got it/them last week.

Tell about your kitchen.
(In my kitchen there's ....)

THE BABY'S ROOM

LA HABITACIÓN DEL/DE LA BEBÉ

osito	**1** teddy bear	sonajero(a)/sonaja/maraquita	**15** rattle
intercomunicador/ monitor de bebé	**2** baby monitor/ intercom	andadera/pollera/andador	**16** walker
ropero/gavetero	**3** chest (of drawers)	cuna/cuna mecedora	**17** cradle
cuna	**4** crib	carriola/cochecito	**18** stroller
móvil	**5** mobile	coche/carricoche	**19** baby carriage
camilla/mesa para cambiar pañales	**6** changing table	asiento para automóvil	**20** car seat/ safety seat
mameluco/pelele/ pijamita de una pieza/mono	**7** stretch suit	portabebé/sillita infantil	**21** baby carrier
cubo/bote/zafacón para pañales	**8** diaper pail	plato térmico para bebés	**22** food warmer
lamparita/lucecita de noche	**9** night light	sillita elevadora	**23** booster seat
baúl para juguetes	**10** toy chest	portabebé/sillita infantil	**24** baby seat
peluche	**11** stuffed animal	trona/silla alta	**25** high chair
muñeca	**12** doll	moisés/cuna portátil	**26** portable crib
columpio	**13** swing	bacinilla/bacenilla/ bacín/bacinica	**27** potty
corral	**14** playpen	portabebé/canguro	**28** baby frontpack
		portabebé	**29** baby backpack

A. Thank you for the **teddy bear**. It's a very nice gift.
B. You're welcome.

A. That's a very nice _____.
   Where did you get it?
B. It was a gift from ....

A. Do you have everything you need
   before the baby comes?
B. Almost everything. We're still looking
   for a/an _____ and a/an _____.

Tell about your country:
   What things do people buy for a new baby?
   Does a new baby sleep in a separate room,
   as in the United States?

THE BATHROOM

EL BAÑO

cesto/canasta	**1** wastebasket		barra para la toalla/ colgador de toallas/toallero	**18** towel rack
gabinete/mueble	**2** vanity		bomba destapacaños/desatascador	**19** plunger
jabón	**3** soap		cepillo	**20** toilet brush
jabonera	**4** soap dish		papel higiénico/sanitario	**21** toilet paper
dispensador de jabón	**5** soap dispenser		desodorante/desodorizador/ aromatizante ambiental	**22** air freshener
lavabo/lavamanos	**6** sink		excusado/retrete/inodoro	**23** toilet
llave/pluma/grifo	**7** faucet		asiento del excusado/redondela	**24** toilet seat
botiquín/gabinete	**8** medicine cabinet		regadera/ducha/baño	**25** shower
espejo	**9** mirror		cortina de baño	**26** shower curtain
vaso	**10** cup		tina/bañera	**27** bathtub/tub
cepillo de dientes	**11** toothbrush		parche antirresbalón/alfombrilla/ estera de goma	**28** rubber mat
cepillo de dientes eléctrico	**12** electric toothbrush		desagüe/escurridor	**29** drain
secadora de cabello/pelo	**13** hair dryer		esponja	**30** sponge
repisa/tablilla	**14** shelf		alfombra/alfombrilla/tapete de baño	**31** bath mat
canasta/cesto para la ropa sucia	**15** hamper		báscula/balanza	**32** scale
ventilador	**16** fan			
toalla	**17** towel			

A. Where's the **hair dryer**?
B. It's *on* the **vanity**.

A. Where's the **soap**?
B. It's *in* the **soap dish**.

A. Where's the **plunger**?
B. It's *next to* the **toilet brush**.

A. [Knock. Knock.] Did I leave my glasses in there?
B. Yes. They're on/in/next to the _____.

A. *Bobby*? You didn't clean up the bathroom! There's toothpaste on the _____, and there's powder all over the _____!
B. Sorry. I'll clean it up right away.

Tell about your bathroom.
(In my bathroom there's ....)

OUTSIDE THE HOME

EL EXTERIOR/FUERA DE LA CASA

El patio delantero	Front Yard	El patio trasero	Backyard
farol	**1** lamppost	silla de jardín	**15** lawn chair
buzón/casilla/casillero postal	**2** mailbox	cortacésped/cortagrama	**16** lawnmower
escalinatas	**3** front steps	barraca/caseta para herramientas	**17** tool shed
porche/portal/soportal	**4** front porch		
contrapuerta	**5** storm door	puerta con tela metálica	**18** screen door
puerta principal	**6** front door	puerta trasera/de atrás	**19** back door
timbre	**7** doorbell	agarrador/tirador/perilla	**20** door knob
ventana	**8** window	patio/cubierta/veranda	**21** deck
malla/tela metálica/mosquitero	**9** window screen	asador/parrilla/barbacoa	**22** barbecue/grill
contraventana/postigo	**10** shutter	patio	**23** patio
tejado/techo	**11** roof	antena parabólica	**24** satellite dish
garaje/estacionamiento/cochera	**12** garage	antena de televisión	**25** TV antenna
puerta del garaje/estacionamiento/de la cochera	**13** garage door	chimenea	**26** chimney
		puerta lateral	**27** side door
entrada para el coche/carro	**14** driveway	cerca(o)/valla	**28** fence

A. When are you going to repair the **lamppost**?
B. I'm going to repair it next Saturday.

[On the telephone]
A. Harry's Home Repairs.
B. Hello. Do you fix _____s?
A. No, we don't.
B. Oh, okay. Thank you.

[At work on Monday morning]
A. What did you do this weekend?
B. Nothing much. I repaired my _____ and my _____.

Do you like to repair things?
What things can you repair yourself?
What things can't you repair? Who repairs them?

EL EDIFICIO DE APARTAMENTOS/DEPARTAMENTOS I

Looking for an Apartment / Búsqueda de apartamentos/departamentos

Búsqueda de apartamentos/departamentos — **Looking for an Apartment**

anuncios/clasificados para apartamentos/departamentos — **1** apartment ads/classified ads

tablero/mural/tablón de anuncios — **2** apartment listings

letrero de vacante — **3** vacancy sign

Firma del contrato — **Signing a Lease**

arrendatario(a)/inquilino(a) — **4** tenant

arrendador(a)/casero(a) — **5** landlord

contrato de alquiler — **6** lease

depósito — **7** security deposit

La mudanza — **Moving In**

camión de mudanzas — **8** moving truck/moving van

vecino(a) — **9** neighbor

conserje — **10** building manager

portero(a) — **11** doorman

llave — **12** key

cerradura/chapa — **13** lock

primer piso — **14** first floor

segundo piso — **15** second floor

tercer piso — **16** third floor

cuarto piso — **17** fourth floor

techo — **18** roof

escalera de emergencia — **19** fire escape

garaje/estacionamiento/aparcamiento con techo — **20** parking garage

balcón — **21** balcony

patio — **22** courtyard

estacionamiento/aparcamiento/parqueadero — **23** parking lot

espacio para estacionarse — **24** parking space

piscina/alberca/pileta — **25** swimming pool

bañera/tina de hidromasaje/de terapia/tina-jacuzzi — **26** whirlpool

basurero — **27** trash bin

aire acondicionado — **28** air conditioner

[19–28]
A. Is there a **fire escape**?
B. Yes, there is.

[14–17]
A. What floor is the apartment on?
B. It's on the _____.

[20, 22–27]
A. Where's the _____?
B. It's in back of the building.

How do people look for apartments in your city or town?

Tell about an apartment building you know:
How many floors are there?
Is there an elevator?
Is there a parking lot or parking garage?
How many apartments are there in the building?

EL EDIFICIO DE APARTAMENTOS/DEPARTAMENTOS II

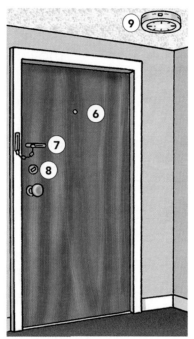

Vestíbulo/Lobby **Lobby**		Pasillo/Corredor **Hallway**	
interfono/portero automático/eléctrico	**1** intercom	salida/escalera de emergencia	**10** fire exit/emergency stairway
timbre/chicharra	**2** buzzer	alarma contra incendios	**11** fire alarm
casilla/casillero postal/buzón	**3** mailbox	superintendente/conserje/encargado(a)	**12** superintendent
ascensor/elevador	**4** elevator	extintor/sistema de aspersión contra incendios	**13** sprinkler system
escalera	**5** stairway	disparador/tobogán/conducto/chuta para la basura	**14** garbage chute/trash chute

Puerta de entrada **Doorway**		Sótano **Basement**	
mirilla	**6** peephole	depósito	**15** storage room
cadena de seguridad/antirrobo	**7** door chain	cuarto de almacenaje	**16** storage locker
cerradura/chapa	**8** lock	lavandería/cuarto de lavado/lavadero	**17** laundry room
detector de humo	**9** smoke detector	verja de seguridad	**18** security gate

[1, 4]

A. Is there an **intercom**?
B. Yes, there is.

[2, 3, 5–18]

A. Is there a **mailbox**?
B. Yes, there is.

[Renting an apartment]
A. Let me show you around.
B. Okay.
A. This is the _____, and here's the _____.
B. I see.

[On the telephone]
A. Mom and Dad? I found an apartment.
B. Good. Tell us about it.
A. It has a/an _____ and a/an _____.
B. That's nice. Does it have a/an _____?
A. Yes, it does.

Do you or someone you know live in an apartment building? Tell about it.

PROBLEMAS DE MANTENIMIENTO Y REPARACIÓN DE LA CASA I

plomero(a)/   **A**   **plumber**
fontanero(a)

El agua de la tina/   **1**   The bathtub is
bañera se sale.   leaking.

El lavabo/lavamanos   **2**   The sink is
está tapado/atascado.   clogged.

El calentador   **3**   The hot water
de agua no funciona.   heater isn't working.

El excusado/retrete/   **4**   The toilet is broken.
inodoro/está
descompuesto.

reparador(a)   **B**   **roofer**
de techos

El techo tiene goteras.   **5**   The roof is leaking.

pintor(a)   **C**   **(house) painter**

La pintura se está   **6**   The paint is
descascarillando.   peeling.

La pared está   **7**   The wall is
cuarteada.   cracked.

compañía de televisión por cable   **D**   **cable TV company**

La señal no funciona.   **8**   The cable TV isn't working.

reparador(a)/mecánico(a)   **E**   **appliance repairperson**
de electrodomésticos

La cocina/estufa no funciona.   **9**   The stove isn't working.

El refrigerador está averiado/   **10**   The refrigerator is
descompuesto.   broken.

fumigador(a)   **F**   **exterminator/**
pest control specialist

Hay ___ en la cocina.   **11**   There are ___ in the kitchen.
carcomas/comejenes/   **a**   termites
termitas/termes

pulgas   **b**   fleas
hormigas   **c**   ants
abejas   **d**   bees
cucarachas   **e**   cockroaches
ratas   **f**   rats
ratones   **g**   mice

A. What's the matter?
B. ___[1–11]___ .
A. I think we should call a/an ___[A–F]___ .

[1–11]
A. I'm having a problem in
my apartment/house.
B. What's the problem?
A. _____ .

[A–F]
A. Can you recommend a good _____?
B. Yes. You should call ....

What do you do when you have these
problems in your home? Do you fix
things yourself, or do you call someone?

HOUSEHOLD PROBLEMS AND REPAIRS II

PROBLEMAS DE MANTENIMIENTO Y REPARACIÓN DE LA CASA II

cerrajero(a) **A locksmith**
La cerradura está rota. **1** The lock is broken.

electricista **B electrician**
La luz de la entrada no **2** The front light
prende/se enciende. doesn't go on.
El timbre de la **3** The doorbell
puerta no suena. doesn't ring.
No hay luz en la sala. **4** The power is out in
the living room.

deshollinador(a) **C chimneysweep**
La chimenea está sucia. **5** The chimney is dirty.

ayudante **D home repairperson/
"handyman"**
Los azulejos del baño **6** The tiles in the
están flojos. bathroom are loose.

carpintero(a) **E carpenter**
Los escalones **7** The steps are
están rotos. broken.
La puerta no **8** The door doesn't
se abre. open.

servicio de calefacción **F heating and air
y aire acondicionado** **conditioning
service**

La calefacción está **9** The heating system
descompuesta/rota. is broken.
El aire acondicionado **10** The air conditioning
no funciona. isn't working.

A. What's the matter?
B. ___[1–10]___ .
A. I think we should call a/an ___[A–F]___ .

[1–10]
A. I'm having a problem in
my apartment/house.
B. What's the problem?
A. _____ .

[A–F]
A. Can you recommend a good _____?
B. Yes. You should call ....

What do you do when you have
these problems in your home? Do
you fix things yourself, or do you call
someone?

LA LIMPIEZA DE LA CASA

barrer el piso	**A** sweep the floor	trapeador seco/mapo/ mopa/mechudo	**9** (dust) mop/ (dry) mop
pasar la aspiradora	**B** vacuum	trapeador de esponja	**10** (sponge) mop
trapear/fregar el piso	**C** mop the floor	trapeador/fregona	**11** (wet) mop
lavar las ventanas	**D** wash the windows	papel toalla/papel absorbente	**12** paper towels
sacudir/quitar el polvo	**E** dust	líquido limpiaventanas	**13** window cleaner
encerar el piso	**F** wax the floor	amoniaco/amoníaco	**14** ammonia
lustrar los muebles	**G** polish the furniture	limpión/trapo para limpiar/sacudir	**15** dust cloth
limpiar el (cuarto de) baño	**H** clean the bathroom	plumero/sacudidor	**16** feather duster
sacar la basura	**I** take out the garbage	cera para el piso	**17** floor wax
		cera para muebles	**18** furniture polish
escoba	**1** broom	limpiador en polvo/farola	**19** cleanser
recogedor	**2** dustpan	cepillo para limpiar el inodoro	**20** scrub brush
escobilla	**3** whisk broom	esponja	**21** sponge
barredor de alfombra	**4** carpet sweeper	cubo/cubeta	**22** bucket/pail
aspiradora	**5** vacuum (cleaner)	basurero/bote para la basura/ tinaco/zafacón	**23** trash can/ garbage can
accesorios para la aspiradora	**6** vacuum cleaner attachments	contenedor de artículos renovables/reciclables	**24** recycling bin
bolsa para la aspiradora	**7** vacuum cleaner bag		
aspiradora de mano	**8** hand vacuum		

[A–I]
A. What are you doing?
B. I'm **sweep**ing **the floor**.

[1–24]
A. I can't find the **broom**.
B. Look over there!

[1–12, 15, 16, 20–24]
A. Excuse me. Do you sell _____(s)?
B. Yes. They're at the back of the store.
A. Thanks.

[13, 14, 17–19]
A. Excuse me. Do you sell _____?
B. Yes. It's at the back of the store.
A. Thanks.

What household cleaning chores do people do in your home? What things do they use?

HERRAMIENTAS Y MATERIALES DE MANTENIMIENTO

martillo	**1** hammer		carretilla	**16** wheelbarrow
serrucho	**2** saw		manguera	**17** hose
destornillador/desarmador	**3** screwdriver		rastrillo	**18** rake
llave/llave para tuercas	**4** wrench		metro/vara de una yarda	**19** yardstick
llave inglesa/ de cremallera/perico	**5** monkey wrench		linterna/lámpara/faro de mano	**20** flashlight
torno/tornillo/ prensa de banco	**6** vise		escalera	**21** ladder
			matamoscas	**22** fly swatter
alicates/pinzas	**7** pliers		bomba/destapacaños	**23** plunger
caja de herramientas	**8** toolbox		trampa para ratones/ ratas/ratonera	**24** mousetrap
taladro eléctrico/barrena	**9** electric drill		insecticida/aerosol para matar insectos	**25** bug spray/ insect spray
clavo	**10** nail		baterías/pilas	**26** batteries
arandela/rondana	**11** washer		foco/bombilla(o)	**27** lightbulbs/bulbs
tuerca	**12** nut		pintura	**28** paint
tornillo	**13** screw		brocha	**29** paintbrush/brush
perno	**14** bolt		rodillo	**30** paint roller
pala	**15** shovel			

A. I can't find the **hammer**!
B. Look in the utility cabinet.
A. Okay. Thanks.

* With 10–14, use: I can't find any _____s.

[1–9, 15–25, 29, 30]
A. Can I borrow your _____?
B. Sure.
A. Thanks.

[10–14, 26, 27]
A. Can I borrow some _____(s)?
B. Sure.
A. Thanks.

What tools and home supplies do you have? How and when do you use them?

EN EL VECINDARIO I

panadería/pastelería/repostería	**1**	bakery
banco	**2**	bank
barbería/peluquería	**3**	barber shop
librería	**4**	book store
terminal de autobuses/camiones	**5**	bus station
guardería infantil	**6**	child-care center/day-care center
tintorería/lavandería en seco	**7**	cleaners
clínica/consultorio	**8**	clinic
tienda de ropa	**9**	clothing store
cafetería/café/cafetín	**10**	coffee shop
tienda de computadoras/ordenadores	**11**	computer store
tienda/tiendita de abarrotes/colmado	**12**	convenience store

A. Where are you going?
B. I'm going to the **bakery**.

A. Are you going to the _____?
B. No. I'm going to the _____.

A. Where did you go?
B. I went to the _____.

Which of these places are in your neighborhood?
(In my neighborhood there's a/an ....)

PLACES AROUND TOWN II

EN EL VECINDARIO II

almacén	**1**	department store
tienda de descuentos	**2**	discount store
churrería/tienda de donas	**3**	donut shop
farmacia/droguería	**4**	drug store/pharmacy
tienda de electrónicos	**5**	electronics store
óptica/oculista	**6**	eye-care center/optician
cafetería/bar/merendero	**7**	fast-food restaurant
floristería/florería/florista	**8**	flower shop/florist
mueblería	**9**	furniture store
gasolinera/surtidor/estación/ bomba de gasolina	**10**	gas station/ service station
tienda/abarrotería/bodega/colmado	**11**	grocery store
salón de belleza/peluquería	**12**	hair salon

A. Hi! How are you today?
B. Fine. Where are you going?
A. To the **department store**. How about you?
B. I'm going to the **discount store**.

A. I'm going to the _____.
B. See you later.
A. Bye.

A. Did you go to the _____ today?
B. No. I went to the _____.

Which of these places are in your neighborhood?
(In my neighborhood there's a/an ....)

ferretería	**1**	hardware store
gimnasio/club	**2**	health club
hospital	**3**	hospital
hotel	**4**	hotel
heladería/refresquería/sorbetería	**5**	ice cream shop
lavandería pública/automática/lavamático	**6**	laundromat
biblioteca	**7**	library
almacén/tienda de ropa de maternidad	**8**	maternity shop
motel	**9**	motel
cine	**10**	movie theater
almacén/tienda de música	**11**	music store
manicurista	**12**	nail salon

A. Where's the **hardware store**?
B. It's right over there.

A. Excuse me. Where's the _____?
B. It's around the corner.
A. Thank you.

A. Excuse me. Is this the way to the _____?
B. Yes, it is.
A. Thanks.

Which of these places are in your neighborhood? (In my neighborhood there's a/an ....)

parque	**1** park		zapatería	**7** shoe store
tienda de mascotas	**2** pet shop		galería/centro comercial	**8** (shopping) mall
pizzería	**3** pizza shop		supermercado	**9** supermarket
oficina de correos	**4** post office		juguetería	**10** toy store
restaurante	**5** restaurant		estación de trenes	**11** train station
escuela/instituto/ colegio	**6** school		videocentro	**12** video store

A. Is there a **park** nearby?
B. Yes. There's a **park** around the corner.

A. Excuse me. Is there a _____ near here?
B. Yes, there is. There's a _____ right over there.
A. Thank you.

A. Oh, no! I can't find my wallet/ purse!
B. Did you leave it at the _____?
A. Maybe I did.

Which of these places are in your neighborhood?
(In my neighborhood there's a/an ....)

THE CITY I

LA CIUDAD I

juzgado/corte/tribunal	**1** courthouse	cárcel	**12** jail
taxi	**2** taxi/cab	acera/banqueta	**13** sidewalk
parada de taxis/piquera	**3** taxi stand	calle	**14** street
taxista/conductor/ chofer de taxi	**4** taxi driver/ cab driver	alumbrado/lámpara/farol/ poste de luz	**15** street light
hidrante/boca de riego	**5** fire hydrant	estacionamiento/parqueadero/ aparcamiento	**16** parking lot
basurero	**6** trash container		
palacio de gobierno/ ayuntamiento/alcaldía	**7** city hall	inspector(a) de estacionómetro/parquímetro	**17** meter maid
alarma contra incendios	**8** fire alarm box	estacionómetro/parquímetro	**18** parking meter
buzón	**9** mailbox	camión de la basura	**19** garbage truck
alcantarilla/desagüe/ drenaje	**10** sewer	subterráneo/metro	**20** subway
estación de policía	**11** police station	estación del metro	**21** subway station

A. Where's the _____?
B. On/In/Next to/Between/Across from/
In front of/Behind/Under/Over the _____.

[1, 11, 12]
A. Excuse me. Where's the _____?
B. It's around the corner.

[3, 6, 8, 9, 16, 21]
A. Excuse me. Is there a _____ nearby?
B. Yes. There's a _____ down the street.

Which of these people, places, and things are in your neighborhood?

THE CITY II

LA CIUDAD II

puesto de periódicos	**1** newsstand	parada/paradero de autobús/ camión	**11** bus stop
semáforo	**2** traffic light	autobús/bus/guagua/camión	**12** bus
cruce/intersección	**3** intersection	conductor(a)/chofer de autobús/busero(a)	**13** bus driver
policía	**4** police officer		
cruce de peatones/ línea de seguridad	**5** crosswalk	edificio de oficinas	**14** office building
peatón(a)	**6** pedestrian	teléfono público	**15** public telephone
repartidor/carretilla de helados/mantecados	**7** ice cream truck	letrero con el nombre de la calle	**16** street sign
		boca de la alcantarilla/ del desagüe/del drenaje	**17** manhole
cuneta/empalme/ bordillo/encintado	**8** curb	motocicleta/moto	**18** motorcycle
estacionamiento/ parqueadero de niveles	**9** parking garage	buhonero/vendedor ambulante	**19** street vendor
estación de bomberos/ bomba	**10** fire station	cajero/ventanilla de servicio rápido	**20** drive-through window

A. Where's the _____?
B. On/In/Next to/Between/Across from/ In front of/Behind/Under/Over the _____.

[4, 13, 19]
A. What do you do?
B. I'm a _____.

[1, 5, 7, 9–11, 14, 15]
A. Excuse me. Is there a/an _____ near here?
B. Yes. There's a/an _____ up the street.

Go to an intersection in your city or town. What do you see? Make a list. Then tell about it. (Use the words on pages 80–83.)

PEOPLE AND PHYSICAL DESCRIPTIONS I

DESCRIPCIÓN FÍSICA DE LAS PERSONAS/LA GENTE I

niño(a)–niños(as)	**1**	**child–children**
bebé/nene(a)	**2**	baby/infant
niño(a) que empieza a andar/ hacer pinitos	**3**	toddler
niño	**4**	boy
niña	**5**	girl
adolescente	**6**	teenager
adulto	**7**	**adult**
hombre–hombres	**8**	man–men
mujer–mujeres	**9**	woman–women
persona mayor/de edad avanzada/ de la tercera edad/anciano(a)	**10**	senior citizen
edad		**age**
joven	**11**	young
maduro(a)/cuarentón(a)/ cincuentón(a)	**12**	middle-aged
mayor/de edad avanzada	**13**	old

estatura	**height**
alto(a)	**14** tall
estatura promedio/mediana	**15** average height
bajo(a)	**16** short
peso	**weight**
gordo(a)	**17** heavy
de peso mediano	**18** average weight
delgado(a)/fino(a)/esbelto(a)	**19** thin/slim
embarazada/encinta	**20** pregnant
discapacitado(a)	**21** physically challenged
ciego(a)/tener problemas de la vista	**22** vision impaired
sordo(a)/tener problemas de oído	**23** hearing impaired

A. Tell me about *your brother*.
B. He's *a tall heavy boy*.

A. Tell me about *your sister*.
B. She's *a short thin girl*.

A. Can you describe the person?
B. I think so.
A. What's *his* age?
B. *He's* ___[11–13]___ .
A. What's *his* height?
B. *He's* ___[14–16]___ .
A. What's *his* weight?
B. *He's* ___[17–19]___ .

Tell about yourself.

Tell about people in your family.

PEOPLE AND PHYSICAL DESCRIPTIONS II

DESCRIPCIÓN FÍSICA DE LAS PERSONAS/LA GENTE II

Descripción del pelo/cabello — Describing Hair

Spanish	#	English
largo	1	long
hasta el hombro	2	shoulder length
corto	3	short
lacio/liso	4	straight
ondulado	5	wavy
rizado/ensortijado/crespo/ encrespado/chino/grifo	6	curly
negro	7	black
café/castaño/marrón	8	brown
rubio/mono/güero	9	blond
pelirrojo	10	red
cano/canoso/gris	11	gray
calvo(a)/pelón(a)	12	bald
barba	13	beard
bigote/mostacho	14	mustache

A. What does *your new boss* look like?
B. *She* has *long straight black* hair.

A. What does *your grandfather* look like?
B. *He* has *short curly gray* hair.

A. Can you describe *his* hair?
B. *He's bald*, and *he* has a *mustache*.

Tell about yourself.   Tell about people in your family.   Tell about your favorite actor or actress or other famous person.

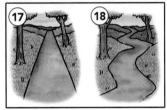

nuevo(a) – viejo(a)	**1–2**	new – old
joven – viejo(a)	**3–4**	young – old
alto(a) – bajo(a)	**5–6**	tall – short
largo(a) – corto(a)	**7–8**	long – short
grande – chiquito(a)/pequeño(a)	**9–10**	large/big – small/little
rápido(a) – lento(a)	**11–12**	fast – slow
gordo(a) – delgado(a)/flaco(a)	**13–14**	heavy/fat – thin/skinny
pesado(a) – liviano(a)	**15–16**	heavy – light
recto(a) – sinuoso(a)/curvo(a)	**17–18**	straight – crooked

liso(a) – rizado(a)/ encrespado(a)	**19–20**	straight – curly
ancho(a) – angosto(a)/ estrecho(a)	**21–22**	wide – narrow
grueso(a) – delgado(a)	**23–24**	thick – thin
oscuro(a) – claro(a)/con luz	**25–26**	dark – light
alto(a) – bajo(a)	**27–28**	high – low
flojo(a)/holgado(a) – estrecho(a)/apretado(a)	**29–30**	loose – tight
bueno(a) – malo(a)	**31–32**	good – bad
caliente – frío(a)	**33–34**	hot – cold
ordenado(a) – desordenado(a)	**35–36**	neat – messy

[1–2]
A. Is your car **new**?
B. No. It's **old**.

1–2 Is your car _____?
3–4 Is he _____?
5–6 Is your sister _____?
7–8 Is his hair _____?
9–10 Is their dog _____?
11–12 Is the train _____?

13–14 Is your friend _____?
15–16 Is the box _____?
17–18 Is the road _____?
19–20 Is her hair _____?
21–22 Is the tie _____?
23–24 Is the line _____?

25–26 Is the room _____?
27–28 Is the bridge _____?
29–30 Are the pants _____?
31–32 Are your neighbor's children _____?
33–34 Is the water _____?
35–36 Is your desk _____?

A. Tell me about your ....
B. He's/She's/It's/They're ____.

A. Do you have a/an ____ ....?
B. No. I have a/an ____ ....

Describe yourself.
Describe a person you know.
Describe some things in your home.
Describe some things in your community.

DESCRIPCIÓN DE PERSONAS/GENTE Y COSAS II

fácil – difícil/duro(a)	**1–2**	easy – difficult/hard	abierto(a) – cerrado(a)	**21–22**	open – closed
suave – duro(a)	**3–4**	soft – hard	lleno(a) – vacío(a)	**23–24**	full – empty
limpio(a) – sucio(a)	**5–6**	clean – dirty	caro(a) – barato(a)	**25–26**	expensive – cheap/inexpensive
terso(a)/liso(a) – áspero(a	**7–8**	smooth – rough			
			elegante – sencillo(a)	**27–28**	fancy – plain
escandaloso(a) – quieto(a)/ tranquilo(a)/callado(a)	**9–10**	noisy/loud – quiet	brillante – opaco(a)	**29–30**	shiny – dull
			afilado(a) – romo(a)/ desafilado(a)	**31–32**	sharp – dull
casado(a) – soltero(a)	**11–12**	married – single	cómodo(a) – incómodo(a)	**33–34**	comfortable – uncomfortable
rico(a) – pobre	**13–14**	rich/wealthy – poor			
bonito(a) – feo(a)	**15–16**	pretty/beautiful – ugly	honesto(a)/honrado(a) – deshonesto(a)	**35–36**	honest – dishonest
guapo(a) – feo(a)	**17–18**	handsome – ugly			
mojado(a) – seco(a)	**19–20**	wet – dry			

[1–2]
A. Is the homework **easy**?
B. No. It's **difficult**.

1–2 Is the homework _____?	13–14 Is your uncle _____?	25–26 Is that restaurant _____?
3–4 Is the mattress _____?	15–16 Is the witch _____?	27–28 Is the dress _____?
5–6 Are the windows _____?	17–18 Is the pirate _____?	29–30 Is your kitchen floor _____?
7–8 Is your skin _____?	19–20 Are the clothes _____?	31–32 Is the knife _____?
9–10 Is your neighbor _____?	21–22 Is the door _____?	33–34 Is the chair _____?
11–12 Is your sister _____?	23–24 Is the pitcher _____?	35–36 Is he _____?

A. Tell me about your ....
B. He's/She's/It's/They're ____.

A. Do you have a/an ____ ....?
B. No. I have a/an ____ ....

Describe yourself.
Describe a person you know.
Describe some things in your home.
Describe some things in your community.

DESCRIBING PHYSICAL STATES AND EMOTIONS I

DESCRIPCIÓN DE ESTADOS FÍSICOS Y EMOTIVOS/DE ÁNIMO I

estar cansado(a)	**1** tired	estar contento(a)	**10** happy
tener sueño/estar soñoliento(a)	**2** sleepy	estar triste	**11** sad/unhappy
		sentirse desgraciado(a)/ infeliz	**12** miserable
estar agotado(a)	**3** exhausted		
estar enfermo(a)	**4** sick/ill	estar entusiasmado(a)/ emocionado (a)	**13** excited
tener calor	**5** hot		**14** disappointed
tener frío	**6** cold	estar decepcionado(a)	
tener hambre	**7** hungry	estar contrariado(a)	**15** upset
tener sed	**8** thirsty	estar molesto(a)/ contrariado(a)	**16** annoyed
estar lleno(a)/ satisfecho(a)	**9** full		

A. You look **tired**.

B. I am. I'm VERY **tired**.

What makes you happy?   What makes you sad?   When do you get annoyed?

DESCRIBING PHYSICAL STATES AND EMOTIONS II

DESCRIPCIÓN DE ESTADOS FÍSICOS Y EMOTIVOS/DE ÁNIMO II

estar enfadado(a)/ disgustado(a)/enojado(a)	**1** angry/mad		estar nervioso(a)	**9** nervous
estar furioso(a)	**2** furious		estar preocupado(a)	**10** worried
estar harto(a)/colmado(a)/ asqueado(a)	**3** disgusted		estar asustado(a)/ tener miedo	**11** scared/ afraid
estar frustrado(a)	**4** frustrated		estar aburrido(a)	**12** bored
estar sorprendido(a)	**5** surprised		estar orgulloso(a)	**13** proud
estar atónito(a)/turbado(a)/ consternado(a)/estupefacto(a)/ pasmado(a)	**6** shocked		estar avergonzado(a)	**14** embarrassed
			estar celoso(a)	**15** jealous
sentirse solo(a)	**7** lonely		estar confundido(a)/ desconcertado(a)/ enredado(a)/ hecho(a) un lío	**16** confused
echar de menos/ tener morriña/nostalgia	**8** homesick			

A. Are you **angry**?
B. Yes. I'm VERY **angry**.

What makes you angry?　　　What makes you nervous?　　　Do you ever feel embarrassed? When?

FRUITS

LAS FRUTAS

manzana	**1** apple	mango	**11** mango	lima/limón (verde)	**21** lime
durazno/ melocotón	**2** peach	higo	**12** fig	naranja/china	**22** orange
pera	**3** pear	coco	**13** coconut	mandarina	**23** tangerine
banana/guineo/ plátano	**4** banana	aguacate	**14** avocado	uvas	**24** grapes
		melón	**15** cantaloupe	cerezas	**25** cherries
plátano verde/ grande	**5** plantain	melón verde/ dulce/chino/de Indias	**16** honeydew (melon)	ciruelas pasas	**26** prunes
ciruela	**6** plum			dátiles	**27** dates
albaricoque/ chabacano/ damasco	**7** apricot	sandía/melón de agua	**17** watermelon	uvas pasas/ pasitas	**28** raisins
		piña	**18** pineapple	nueces	**29** nuts
nectarina	**8** nectarine	toronja/ pomelo	**19** grapefruit	frambuesas	**30** raspberries
kiwi	**9** kiwi			arándanos	**31** blueberries
papaya/fruta bomba	**10** papaya	lima/limón (amarillo)	**20** lemon	fresas	**32** strawberries

[1–23]
A. This **apple** is delicious!
B. I'm glad you like it.

[24–32]
A. These **grapes** are delicious!
B. I'm glad you like them.

A. I'm hungry. Do we have any fruit?
B. Yes. We have _____s* and _____s.*

* With 15–19, use: We have _____ and _____.

A. Do we have any more _____s?†
B. No. I'll get some more when I go to the supermarket.

† With 15–19, use:
   Do we have any more _____?

What are your favorite fruits?
Which fruits don't you like?

Which of these fruits grow where you live?

Name and describe other fruits you know.

VEGETABLES

LOS VEGETALES/LAS VERDURAS

apio	**1**	celery	guisante/chícharo/ petit pois	**16**	pea	batata dulce/ camote	**29**	sweet potato
maíz/elote	**2**	corn	habichuelas tiernas/ ejotes/judías verdes	**17**	string bean/ green bean	batata (anaranjada)	**30**	yam
brécol/brócoli	**3**	broccoli	haba	**18**	lima bean	pimiento verde	**31**	green pepper/ sweet pepper
coliflor	**4**	cauliflower	frijol negro	**19**	black bean			
espinaca	**5**	spinach	frijol rojo/colorado/ habichuela colorada/poroto	**20**	kidney bean	pimiento rojo/ pimiento morrón	**32**	red pepper
perejil	**6**	parsley	repollito/ col de bruselas	**21**	brussels sprout	chile/pimiento jalapeño	**33**	jalapeño (pepper)
espárragos	**7**	asparagus	pepino/pepinillo	**22**	cucumber	chile colorado	**34**	chili pepper
berenjena	**8**	eggplant	tomate/jitomate	**23**	tomato	remolacha/ betabel	**35**	beet
lechuga	**9**	lettuce	zanahoria	**24**	carrot	cebolla	**36**	onion
repollo/col	**10**	cabbage	rábano	**25**	radish	cebollino(a)/ cebollín/ escalonia	**37**	scallion/ green onion
bok choy	**11**	bok choy	hongo/seta/ champiñón	**26**	mushroom	nabo	**38**	turnip
calabacita/ calabacín	**12**	zucchini	alcachofa	**27**	artichoke			
calabaza pequeña	**13**	acorn squash	papa/patata	**28**	potato			
zapallo/ güira(o)	**14**	butternut squash						
ajo	**15**	garlic						

A. What do we need from the supermarket?
B. We need **celery*** and **pea**s.†

* 1–15   † 16–38

A. How do you like the
   ___[1–15]___?
B. It's delicious.

A. How do you like the
   ___[16–38]___s?
B. They're delicious.

Which vegetables do you like?
Which vegetables don't you like?

Which of these vegetables grow where you live?

Name and describe other vegetables you know.

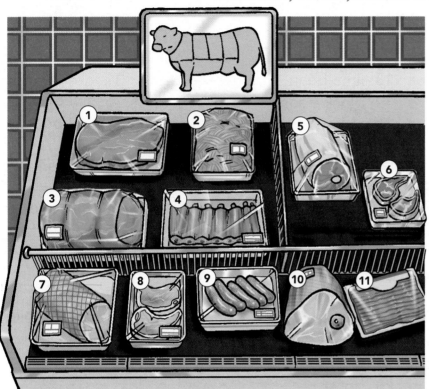

Carnes	Meat		Aves	Poultry		Pescados y mariscos	Seafood
filete/bistec/bisté/bife	**1** steak		pollo/gallina	**12** chicken		PESCADOS FISH	
carne molida	**2** ground beef		pechugas de pollo/gallina	**13** chicken breasts		salmón	**19** salmon
carne para asar	**3** roast beef		muslos de pollo/gallina	**14** chicken legs/drumsticks		mero	**20** halibut
costillas	**4** ribs		alitas/alas de pollo/gallina	**15** chicken wings		abadejo/bacalao	**21** haddock
pierna de cordero	**5** leg of lamb		encuentros/caderas de pollo/gallina	**16** chicken thighs		lenguado	**22** flounder
chuletas de cordero	**6** lamb chops					trucha	**23** trout
puerco/cerdo	**7** pork		pavo/guajolote	**17** turkey		bagro/bagre/barbo	**24** catfish
chuletas de puerco/cerdo	**8** pork chops		pato	**18** duck		filete de lenguado/de suela	**25** filet of sole
salchichones/chorizos/longaniza/salchichas	**9** sausages					MARISCOS SHELLFISH	
jamón	**10** ham					gambas/langostinos/camarones	**26** shrimp
tocino/tocineta/panceta/bacón/beicon	**11** bacon					conchuelas/vieiras/veneras/callos de hacha	**27** scallops
						almejas	**28** clams
						cangrejos	**29** crabs
						langosta	**30** lobster

[1–11]

A. Excuse me. Where can I find **steak**?
B. Look in the Meat Section.
A. Thank you.

[12–18]

A. Excuse me. Where can I find **chicken**?
B. Look in the Poultry Section.
A. Thank you.

[19–30]

A. Excuse me. Where can I find **salmon**?
B. Look in the Seafood Section.
A. Thank you.

[1–3, 5, 7, 10–12, 17–25, 30]

A. This _____ looks very fresh!
B. Let's get some for dinner.

[4, 6, 8, 9, 13–16, 26–29]

A. These _____ look very fresh!
B. Let's get some for dinner.

Do you eat meat, poultry, or seafood?
Which of these foods do you like?

Which of these foods are popular in your country?

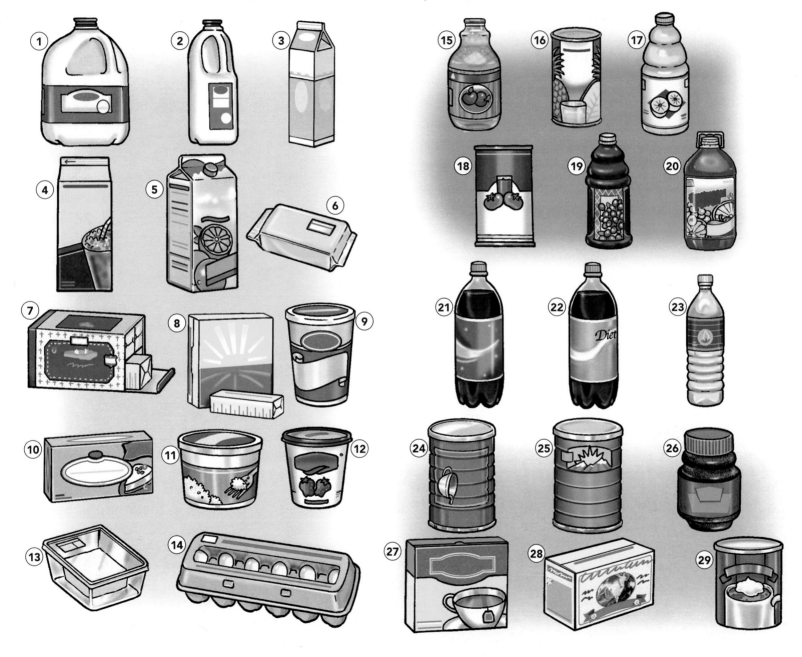

Productos lácteos	Dairy Products	Jugos/Zumos	Juices	Café y té	Coffee and Tea
leche	**1** milk	jugo de manzana	**15** apple juice	café	**24** coffee
leche baja en grasa	**2** low-fat milk	jugo de piña	**16** pineapple juice	café descafeinado	**25** decaffeinated coffee/decaf
leche descremada/ desgrasada	**3** skim milk	jugo de toronja/ pomelo	**17** grapefruit juice	café instantáneo	**26** instant coffee
leche con chocolate	**4** chocolate milk			té	**27** tea
jugo de naranja/ china	**5** orange juice*	jugo de tomate	**18** tomato juice	tisana/infusión de hierbas/ yerbas	**28** herbal tea
queso	**6** cheese	jugo de uvas	**19** grape juice		
mantequilla	**7** butter	ponche de frutas	**20** fruit punch	chocolate en polvo	**29** cocoa/ hot chocolate mix
margarina	**8** margarine				
crema agria/crema	**9** sour cream	**Bebidas**	**Beverages**		
queso crema	**10** cream cheese	soda/gaseosa/ refresco	**21** soda		
requesón/cuajada	**11** cottage cheese				
yogur/leche búlgara	**12** yogurt	soda de dieta	**22** diet soda		
soja/soya/tofu*	**13** tofu*	agua embotellada	**23** bottled water		
huevos	**14** eggs				

* El jugo de naranja y el tofu no son productos lácteos, pero usualmente se les encuentra en esta sección.

A. I'm going to the supermarket to get some **milk**. Do we need anything else?

B. Yes. Please get some **apple juice**.

A. Excuse me. Where can I find _____?

B. Look in the _____ Section.

A. Thanks.

A. Look! _____ is on sale this week!

B. Let's get some!

* With 14, use: _____ are on sale this week.

Which of these foods do you like?

Which of these foods are good for you?

Which brands of these foods do you buy?

DELICATESSEN/CHARCUTERÍA, CARNES FRÍAS, PRODUCTOS CONGELADOS Y APERITIVOS

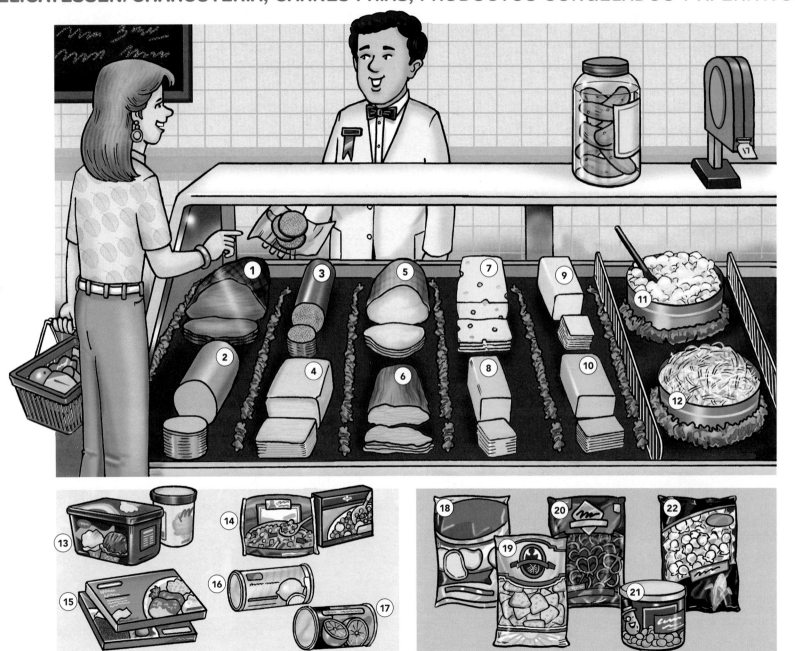

Delicatessen/Charcutería — Deli

carne (de vaca) asada/rosbif	**1**	roast beef
mortadela	**2**	bologna
salami	**3**	salami
jamón	**4**	ham
pavo/guajolote	**5**	turkey
carne adobada/ en salmuera/ salpresa/cornbif	**6**	corned beef
queso suizo	**7**	Swiss cheese
queso americano	**8**	American cheese
mozzarella	**9**	mozzarella
queso cheddar	**10**	cheddar cheese
ensalada de papas/ patatas	**11**	potato salad
ensalada de repollo/col	**12**	cole slaw

Productos congelados — Frozen Foods

helado	**13**	ice cream
vegetales congelados	**14**	frozen vegetables
comida congelada/platos congelados	**15**	frozen dinners
concentrado de limonada congelada	**16**	frozen lemonade
concentrado de jugo de naranja/china congelado	**17**	frozen orange juice

Aperitivos/Botanas/Antojitos/Pasabocas — Snack Foods

papas/papitas/patatas fritas	**18**	potato chips
fritos de tortilla/ totoposte/totopo	**19**	tortilla chips
pretzels	**20**	pretzels
nueces	**21**	nuts
palomitas/rosetas/ hojuelas/rositas de maíz	**22**	popcorn

A. Should we get some **roast beef**?
B. Good idea. And let's get some **potato salad**.

[1–12]
A. May I help you?
B. Yes, please. I'd like some _____.

[1–22]
A. Excuse me. Where is/are _____?
B. It's/They're in the _____ Section.

Which of these foods do you like?

Which brands of these foods do you buy?

ABARROTES/PROVISIONES

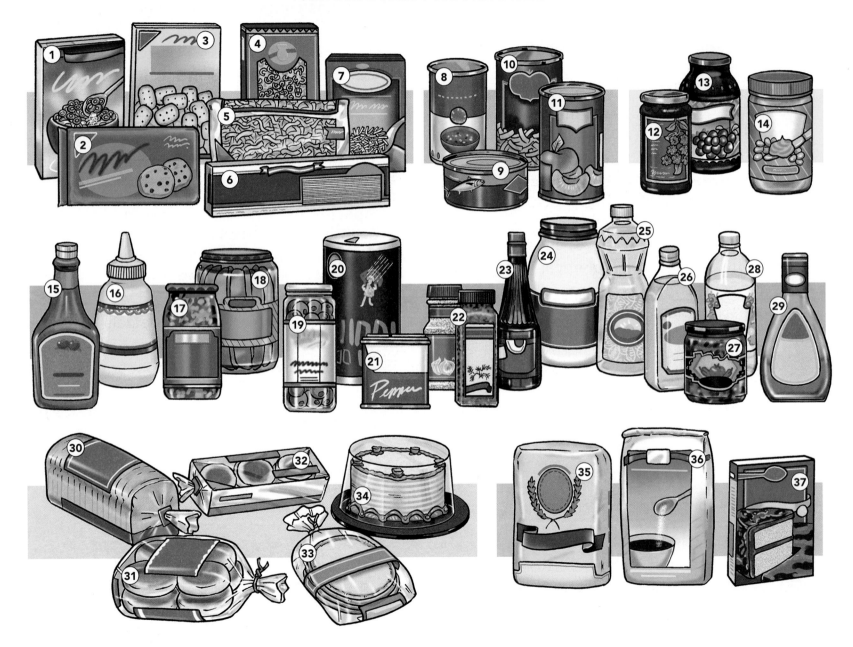

Productos envasados/ empaquetados	Packaged Goods				
cereal	**1** cereal	mantequilla de maní/cacahuete/ cacahuate/crema de cacahuate	**14** peanut butter	aceite de oliva	**26** olive oil
galletas	**2** cookies			salsa	**27** salsa
galletas saladas/de soda	**3** crackers			vinagre	**28** vinegar
coditos/macarrones cortos	**4** macaroni	**Condimentos/ especias y salsas**	**Condiments**	sazón/aliño/ aderezo para ensaladas	**29** salad dressing
fideos/tallarines	**5** noodles	salsa de tomate/ catsup	**15** ketchup		
espaguetis	**6** spaghetti	mostaza	**16** mustard	**Panadería y pastelería**	**Baked Goods**
arroz	**7** rice	encurtido picado	**17** relish	pan	**30** bread
		encurtidos	**18** pickles	bollos/panecillos	**31** rolls
Productos enlatados	**Canned Goods**	aceitunas	**19** olives	bollos/panecillos	**32** English muffins
sopa	**8** soup	sal	**20** salt		
atún enlatado	**9** tuna (fish)	pimienta	**21** pepper	pan de pita	**33** pita bread
vegetales/verduras enlatados(as)	**10** (canned) vegetables	especias/ condimentos	**22** spices	bizcocho/torta/ pastel/ponqué	**34** cake
fruta enlatada	**11** (canned) fruit	salsa china/ de soja/soya	**23** soy sauce	**Productos para hornear**	**Baking Products**
Mermeladas y confituras	**Jams and Jellies**	mayonesa	**24** mayonnaise	harina	**35** flour
mermelada	**12** jam	aceite para cocinar	**25** (cooking) oil	azúcar	**36** sugar
jalea	**13** jelly			harina preparada para bizcocho	**37** cake mix

A. I got **cereal** and **soup**. What else is on the shopping list?
B. **Ketchup** and **bread**.

A. Excuse me. I'm looking for _____.
B. It's/They're next to the _____.

A. Pardon me. I'm looking for _____.
B. It's/They're between the _____ and the _____.

Which of these foods do you like?

Which brands of these foods do you buy?

ARTÍCULOS PARA EL HOGAR, EL/LA BEBÉ Y LAS MASCOTAS

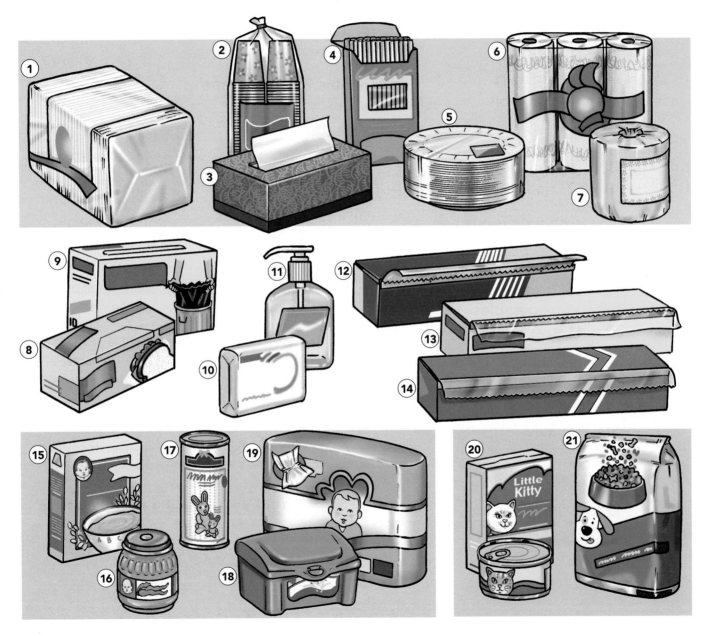

Productos de papel/ desechables		Paper Products
servilletas	**1**	napkins
vasos de cartón/desechables	**2**	paper cups
pañuelos desechables/kleenex	**3**	tissues
pajillas/popotes/ carrizos/sorbetos	**4**	straws
platos de cartón/ desechables	**5**	paper plates
papel toalla	**6**	paper towels
papel higiénico/sanitario	**7**	toilet paper

Artículos para el hogar		Household Items
bolsitas plásticas para sándwiches	**8**	sandwich bags
bolsas para la basura	**9**	trash bags
jabón	**10**	soap

jabón líquido	**11**	liquid soap
papel de aluminio	**12**	aluminum foil
plástico para envolver	**13**	plastic wrap
papel encerado/de cera	**14**	waxed paper

Artículos para el bebé		Baby Products
cereal	**15**	baby cereal
papillas/colados	**16**	baby food
fórmula	**17**	formula
toallitas húmedas desechables	**18**	wipes
pañales desechables	**19**	(disposable) diapers

Comida para mascotas		Pet Food
comida para gatos	**20**	cat food
comida para perros	**21**	dog food

A. Excuse me. Where can I find **napkins**?
B. **Napkins**? Look in Aisle 4.

[7, 10–17, 20, 21]
A. We forgot to get _____!
B. I'll get it. Where is it?
A. It's in Aisle _____.

[1–6, 8, 9, 18, 19]
A. We forgot to get _____!
B. I'll get them. Where are they?
A. They're in Aisle _____.

What do you need from the supermarket?
Make a complete shopping list!

EL SUPERMERCADO

pasillo/corredor	**1** aisle		caja rápida	**12** express checkout (line)
cliente(a)	**2** shopper/customer		lector óptico	**13** scanner
carretilla/carrito	**3** shopping basket		bolsa plástica/de plástico	**14** plastic bag
fila para pagar	**4** checkout line			
mostrador de chequeo/caja	**5** checkout counter		gerente	**15** manager
caja registradora	**6** cash register		empleado(a)	**16** clerk
carrito/carretilla	**7** shopping cart		pesa/balanza	**17** scale
cupones	**8** coupons		recicladora/reembolsadora para latas	**18** can-return machine
cajero(a)	**9** cashier			
bolsa/cartucho/talego de papel	**10** paper bag		recicladora/reembolsadora para botellas	**19** bottle-return machine
empacador(a)	**11** bagger/packer			

A. This is a gigantic supermarket!
B. It is! Look at all the **aisle**s!

Where do you usually shop for food? Do you go to a supermarket, or do you go to a small grocery store? Describe the place where you shop.

Describe the differences between U.S. supermarkets and food stores in your country.

ENVASES/RECIPIENTES Y MEDIDAS DE CANTIDAD

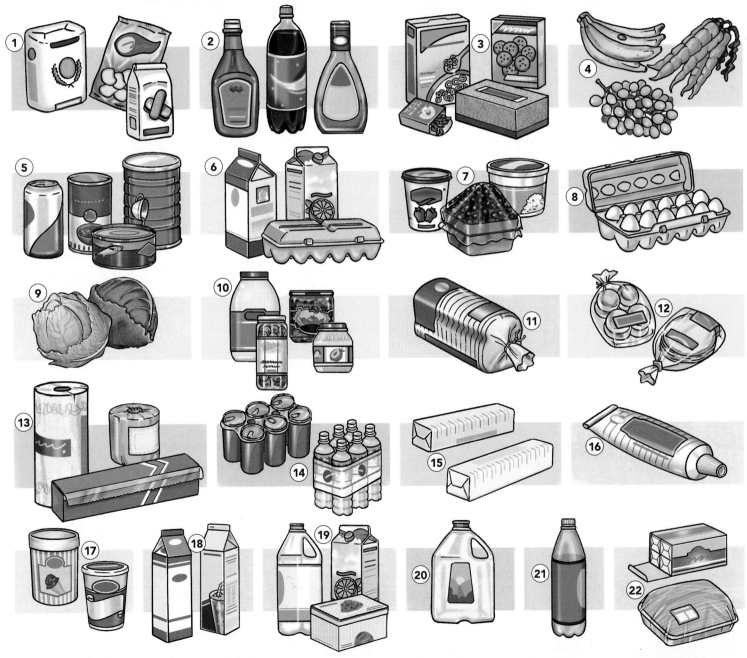

bolsa	**1** bag	cabeza	**9** head	barra	**15** stick
botella	**2** bottle	frasco/tarro/	**10** jar	tubo	**16** tube
caja/cajeta/	**3** box	pote		pinta	**17** pint
cajetita		hogaza(s)/	**11** loaf/loaves	cuarto de	**18** quart
racimo/	**4** bunch	barra(s) de pan		galón	
manojo/mazo		paquete/bulto	**12** package	medio galón	**19** half-gallon
lata	**5** can	rollo	**13** roll	galón	**20** gallon
cartón	**6** carton	cartón/paquete/	**14** six-pack	litro	**21** liter
envase	**7** container	bulto de seis		libra	**22** pound
docena	**8** dozen*	artículos			

* "a dozen eggs," NO "a dozen of eggs"

A. Please get a **bag** of *flour* when you go to the supermarket.
B. A **bag** of *flour*? Okay.

A. Please get two **bottles** of *ketchup* when you go to the supermarket.
B. Two **bottles** of *ketchup*? Okay.

[At home]

A. What did you get at the supermarket?
B. I got ____, ____, and ____.

[In a supermarket]

A. This is the express checkout line. Do you have more than eight items?
B. No. I only have ____, ____, and ____.

Open your kitchen cabinets and refrigerator. Make a list of all the things you find.

What do you do with empty bottles, jars, and cans? Do you recycle them, reuse them, or throw them away?

PESOS Y MEDIDAS I

cucharadita **teaspoon**
cdta. **tsp.**

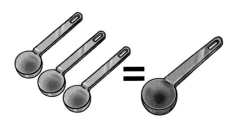

cucharada **tablespoon**
cda. **Tbsp.**

una onza **1 (fluid) ounce**
1 oz. líquida **1 fl. oz.**

una taza **cup**
  c.
8 oz. **8 fl. ozs.**
líquidas

una pinta **pint**
  pt.
16 oz. **16 fl. ozs.**
líquidas

un cuarto de galón **quart**
  qt.
32 oz. líquidas **32 fl. ozs.**

un galón **gallon**
  gal.
128 oz. **128 fl. ozs.**
líquidas

A. How much water should I put in?
B. The recipe says to add one _____ of water.

A. This fruit punch is delicious! What's in it?
B. Two _____s of apple juice, three _____
of orange juice, and a _____ of grape juice.

PESOS Y MEDIDAS II

una onza	an ounce	un cuarto de libra	a quarter of a pound	media libra	half a pound	tres cuartos de libra	three-quarters of a pound	una libra	a pound
		¼ lb.	1/4 lb.	½ lb.	1/2 lb.	¾ lb.	3/4 lb.	1 lb.	lb.
1 oz.	oz.	4 oz.	4 ozs.	8 oz.	8 ozs.	12 oz.	12 ozs.	16 oz.	16 ozs.

A. How much roast beef would you like?

B. I'd like _____, please.

A. Anything else?

B. Yes. Please give me _____ of Swiss cheese.

A. This chili tastes very good! What did you put in it?

B. _____ of ground beef, _____ of beans, _____ of tomatoes, and _____ of chili powder.

FOOD PREPARATION AND RECIPES

RECETAS Y PREPARACIÓN DE ALIMENTOS

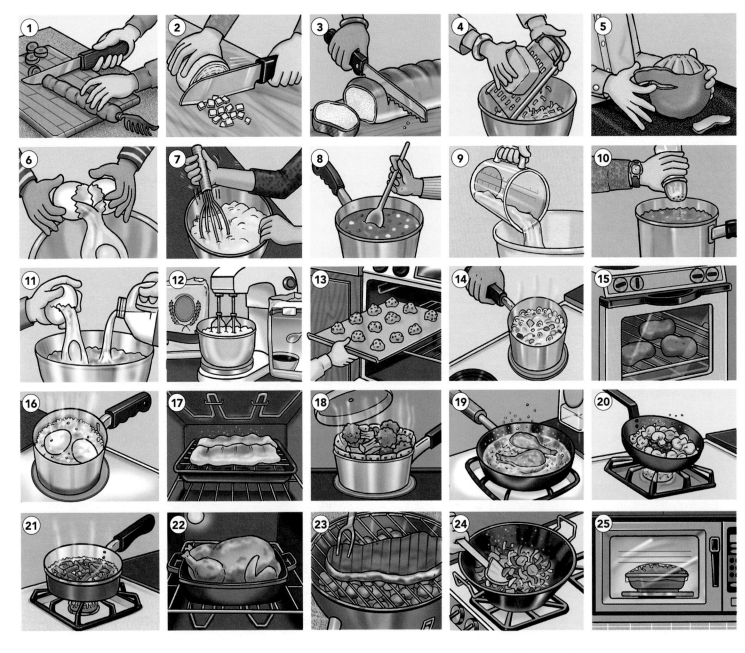

corte(a)	**1**	cut (up)	cocine(a)	**14**	cook
pique (pica)	**2**	chop (up)	hornee(a)	**15**	bake
corte(a)/rebane(a)	**3**	slice	hierva(e)	**16**	boil
ralle(a)	**4**	grate	ase(a) a la parrilla	**17**	broil
pele(a)/monde(a)	**5**	peel	cuezca/cueza (cuece) al vapor	**18**	steam
parta(e)	**6**	break	fría(e)	**19**	fry
bata(e)	**7**	beat	guise(a)/saltee(a)	**20**	saute
revuelva(e)	**8**	stir	cuezca/cueza (cuece) a fuego lento	**21**	simmer
eche(a)/vierta(e)	**9**	pour	ase(a)/hornee(a)	**22**	roast
añada(e)	**10**	add	ase(a) a la parrilla	**23**	barbecue/grill
combine(a) ___ y ___	**11**	combine ___ and ___	saltee(a)/sofría(e)	**24**	stir-fry
mezcle(a) ___ y ___	**12**	mix ___ and ___	cuezca/cueza (cuece)/	**25**	microwave
ponga (pon) ___ en ___	**13**	put ___ in ___	cocine(a) en el microondas		

A. Can I help you?
B. Yes. Please **cut up** the vegetables.

[1–25]
A. What are you doing?
B. I'm _____ing the ....

[14–25]
A. How long should I _____ the ....?
B. _____ the .... for .... minutes/seconds.

What's your favorite recipe? Give instructions and use the units of measure on pages 114 and 115. For example:

Mix a cup of flour and two tablespoons of sugar.
Add half a pound of butter.
Bake at 350° (degrees) for twenty minutes.

FAST FOOD

COMIDA RÁPIDA/AL PASO/AL INSTANTE

hamburguesa	**1**	hamburger	helado	**14**	ice cream
hamburguesa con queso/ quesoburguesa	**2**	cheeseburger	helado de yogur	**15**	frozen yogurt
perro caliente/hot dog	**3**	hot dog	batido de leche/malteada	**16**	milkshake
bocadillo/emparedado/ sándwich de pescado	**4**	fish sandwich	soda/gaseosa	**17**	soda
bocadillo/emparedado/ sándwich de pollo	**5**	chicken sandwich	tapas	**18**	lids
pollo frito	**6**	fried chicken	vasos de cartón	**19**	paper cups
papas fritas	**7**	french fries	pajillas/popotes/carrizos/sorbetos	**20**	straws
nachos	**8**	nachos	servilletas	**21**	napkins
taco	**9**	taco	cubiertos plásticos/de plástico	**22**	plastic utensils
burrito	**10**	burrito	salsa de tomate/catsup	**23**	ketchup
pedazo de pizza	**11**	slice of pizza	mostaza	**24**	mustard
tazón de chile con carne	**12**	bowl of chili	mayonesa	**25**	mayonnaise
ensalada	**13**	salad	encurtido de pepinillos	**26**	relish
			sazón/aliño/ aderezo para ensaladas	**27**	salad dressing

A. May I help you?
B. Yes. I'd like a/an ___[1–5, 9–17]___ / an order of ___[6–8]___ .

A. Excuse me. We're almost out of ___[18–27]___ .
B. I'll get some more from the supply room. Thanks for telling me.

Do you go to fast-food restaurants? Which ones? How often? What do you order?

Are there fast-food restaurants in your country? Are they popular? What foods do they have?

churro/dona/buñuelo/llanta	**1** donut	té frío/helado	**16** iced tea
pan dulce/bollo/bollito	**2** muffin	limonada	**17** lemonade
bagel	**3** bagel	chocolate caliente	**18** hot chocolate
pan dulce danés	**4** danish/pastry	leche	**19** milk
bisquet/panecillo	**5** biscuit	bocadillo/emparedado/ sándwich de atún	**20** tuna fish sandwich
croissant/cuernito	**6** croissant	bocadillo/emparedado/ sándwich de huevo	**21** egg salad sandwich
huevos	**7** eggs	bocadillo/emparedado/ sándwich de pollo	**22** chicken salad sandwich
panqueques/hot cakes	**8** pancakes	bocadillo/emparedado/ sándwich de jamón con queso	**23** ham and cheese sandwich
waffles/gofres	**9** waffles	bocadillo/emparedado/ sándwich de tomate con lechuga y tocino	**24** BLT/bacon, lettuce, and tomato sandwich
pan tostado/tostada	**10** toast		
tocino/tocineta	**11** bacon		
chorizos/salchichas	**12** sausages		
café	**13** coffee		
café descafeinado	**14** decaf coffee		
té	**15** tea		

A. May I help you?
B. Yes. I'd like a ___[1–6]___ /an order of ___[7–12]___ , please.
A. Anything to drink?
B. Yes. I'll have a small/medium-size/large/ extra-large ___[13–19]___ .

A. I'd like a ___[20–24]___ , please.
B. What do you want on it?
A. Lettuce/tomato/mayonnaise/mustard/...

Do you like these foods? Which ones? Where do you get them? How often do you have them?

EL RESTAURANTE I

lleve los/las clientes(as) a la mesa	**A** seat the customers	asiento elevador	**7** booster seat
vierta/sirva el agua	**B** pour the water	menú/carta	**8** menu
tome/anote la orden	**C** take the order	canasta/canastilla/ cesta para pan	**9** bread basket
sirva la comida	**D** serve the meal	ayudante de camarero(a)	**10** busperson
anfitriona	**1** hostess	mesera/camarera	**11** waitress/server
anfitrión	**2** host	mesero/camarero	**12** waiter/server
cliente(a)/comensal	**3** diner/customer	barra de ensaladas	**13** salad bar
butaca/reservado/privado	**4** booth	comedor	**14** dining room
mesa	**5** table	cocina	**15** kitchen
silla alta/trona	**6** high chair	chef	**16** chef

[A–D]

A. Please **seat the customers**.

B. All right. I'll **seat the customers** right away.

[1, 2, 10–12, 16]

A. Do you have any job openings?

B. Yes. We're looking for a **hostess**.

[4–9]

A. Would you like a **booth**?

B. Yes, please.

[13–16]

A. This restaurant has a wonderful **salad bar**.

B. I agree.

Tell about a restaurant you know. Describe the place and the people. (Is the restaurant large or small? How many tables are there? How many people work there? Is there a salad bar? . . .)

EL RESTAURANTE II

limpie la mesa	**A** clear the table	cuenta	**5** check	platito/platillo	**14** saucer
pague la cuenta	**B** pay the check	propina	**6** tip	servilleta	**15** napkin
deje una propina	**C** leave a tip	plato para la ensalada	**7** salad plate	**juego de cubiertos/ cuchillería**	**silverware**
ponga/arregle la mesa	**D** set the table	plato para el pan y la mantequilla	**8** bread-and-butter plate	tenedor/trinche para la ensalada	**16** salad fork
cuarto para lavar platos	**1** dishroom	plato llano	**9** dinner plate	tenedor	**17** dinner fork
lavaplatos/ lavavajillas	**2** dishwasher	plato hondo/ sopero	**10** soup bowl	cuchillo	**18** knife
bandeja/charola	**3** tray	vaso/copa para el agua	**11** water glass	cucharita/cucharilla/ cuchara de té	**19** teaspoon
carrito de postres	**4** dessert cart	copa	**12** wine glass	cuchara para la sopa	**20** soup spoon
		taza	**13** cup	cuchillo para la mantequilla	**21** butter knife

[A–D]

A. Please **clear the table**.
B. All right. I'll **clear the table** right away.

[7–21]

A. Excuse me. Where does the **salad fork** go?
B. It goes *to the left of* the **dinner fork**.

A. Excuse me. Where does the **bread-and-butter plate** go?
B. It goes *to the right of* the **salad plate**.

A. Excuse me. Where does the **cup** go?
B. It goes *on* the **saucer**.

A. Excuse me. Where does the **teaspoon** go?
B. It goes *between* the **knife** and the **soup spoon**.

Practice giving directions. Tell someone how to set a table. (Put the . . . . . .)

A RESTAURANT MENU

UN MENÚ

coctel/copa de frutas	**1** fruit cup	alitas de pollo	**4** chicken wings
jugo de tomate	**2** tomato juice	nachos	**5** nachos
coctel de camarones/gambas	**3** shrimp cocktail	papas rellenas	**6** potato skins

ensalada mixta	**7** tossed salad	una papa al horno/asada	**18** a baked potato
ensalada griega	**8** Greek salad	puré de papas	**19** mashed potatoes
ensalada de espinacas	**9** spinach salad	papas fritas	**20** french fries
antipasto/entremés	**10** antipasto (plate)	arroz	**21** rice
ensalada estilo César	**11** Caesar salad	fideos	**22** noodles
		vegetales/verduras mixtas(os)	**23** mixed vegetables
pastel/budín de carne molida	**12** meatloaf	bizcocho/torta/ pastel de chocolate	**24** chocolate cake
filete/bistec de costilla/ asado/bife/rosbif	**13** roast beef	pastel/tarta de manzana	**25** apple pie
pollo al horno/asado	**14** baked chicken	helado	**26** ice cream
pescado a la parrilla	**15** broiled fish	gelatina	**27** jello
espaguetis con albóndigas	**16** spaghetti and meatballs	pudín/budín	**28** pudding
chuleta de ternera	**17** veal cutlet	copa de helado/mantecado especial/sundae	**29** ice cream sundae

[Ordering dinner]

A. May I take your order?
B. Yes, please. For the appetizer, I'd like the ___[1–6]___.
A. And what kind of salad would you like?
B. I'll have the ___[7–11]___.
A. And for the main course?
B. I'd like the ___[12–17]___, please.
A. What side dish would you like with that?
B. Hmm. I think I'll have ___[18–23]___.

[Ordering dessert]

A. Would you like some dessert?
B. Yes. I'll have ___[24–28]___ /an ___[29]___.

Tell about the food at a restaurant you know.
What's on the menu?

What are some typical foods on the menus of restaurants in your country?

COLORS

LOS COLORES

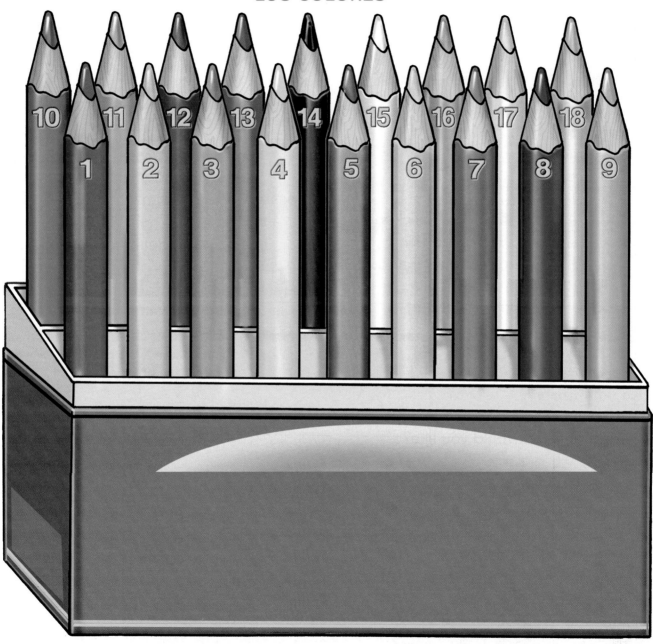

rojo	**1**	red	verde	**10**	green
rosado/rosa	**2**	pink	verde claro	**11**	light green
anaranjado/naranja	**3**	orange	verde oscuro	**12**	dark green
amarillo	**4**	yellow	morado/violeta	**13**	purple
marrón/chocolate/	**5**	brown	negro	**14**	black
pardo/café/carmelita			blanco	**15**	white
crema/beige	**6**	beige	gris	**16**	gray
azul	**7**	blue	plateado/plata	**17**	silver
azul marino	**8**	navy blue	dorado/oro	**18**	gold
turquesa	**9**	turquoise			

A. What's your favorite color?
B. **Red**.

A. I like your _____ shirt.
 You look very good in _____.
B. Thank you. _____ is my
 favorite color.

A. My TV is broken.
B. What's the matter with it?
A. People's faces are _____,
 the sky is _____, and the
 grass is _____!

Do you know the flags of different countries?
What are the colors of flags you know?

What color makes you happy? What color
makes you sad? Why?

CLOTHING

LA ROPA

blusa	**1** blouse	corbata	**14** tie
falda	**2** skirt	uniforme	**15** uniform
camisa	**3** shirt	camiseta/playera	**16** T-shirt
pantalones	**4** pants/slacks	pantalones cortos/shorts	**17** shorts
camisa de mangas cortas	**5** sport shirt	vestido/traje de maternidad	**18** maternity dress
pantalones vaqueros/jeans/ de mezclilla/mahones	**6** jeans	mono/mameluco/overol/guardapolvo	**19** jumpsuit
polo/camisa/jersey de punto	**7** knit shirt/jersey	chaleco	**20** vest
vestido/traje	**8** dress	mameluco/trajecito júmper/mono	**21** jumper
suéter/con cuello de pico	**9** sweater	túnica	**22** tunic
chaqueta/saco	**10** jacket	leotardos/mallas	**23** leggings
chaqueta/saco informal/ deportiva(o)/chaquetón/ campera/americana	**11** sport coat/ sport jacket	overol/mono/mameluco	**24** overalls
		camisa de cuello de tortuga/cisne	**25** turtleneck
		esmoquin/smóking	**26** tuxedo
traje sastre/vestido de chaqueta/de dos piezas	**12** suit	corbata de gato/de lazo/ de pajarita/mariquita/corbatín	**27** bow tie
conjunto/traje de tres piezas/terno	**13** three-piece suit	vestido/traje de noche/de fiesta/ formal/de etiqueta	**28** (evening) gown

A. I think I'll wear my new **blouse** today.
B. Good idea!

A. I really like your _____.
B. Thank you.
A. Where did you get it/them?
B. At ....

A. Oh, no! I just ripped my _____!
B. What a shame!

What clothing items in this lesson do you wear?

What color clothing do you like to wear?

What do you wear at work or at school? at parties? at weddings?

OUTERWEAR

ROPA PARA RESGUARDARSE DEL TIEMPO

abrigo/gabán/sobretodo	**1** coat	paraguas/parasol/sombrilla	**15** umbrella
abrigo/gabán/sobretodo	**2** overcoat	poncho (de agua)/jorongo/sarape	**16** poncho
sombrero	**3** hat	capote corto/chamarra para lluvia/chubasquero	**17** rain jacket
chaqueta/cazadora/chompa/chamarra	**4** jacket	botas de goma/caucho/hule/para la lluvia	**18** rain boots
bufanda	**5** scarf	gorro(a) de esquiar	**19** ski hat
abrigo tejido/de punto	**6** sweater jacket	abrigo/chaqueta de esquiar	**20** ski jacket
leotardos/mallas	**7** tights	guantes	**21** gloves
gorra/cachucha	**8** cap	máscara de esquiar/pasamontañas	**22** ski mask
chaqueta de cuero	**9** leather jacket	abrigo/chaqueta de plumas de ganso/acolchonado(a)	**23** down jacket
gorra de béisbol	**10** baseball cap	mitones/guantes enteros	**24** mittens
chaqueta/impermeable contra el viento	**11** windbreaker	abrigo de invierno/pelliza/parka	**25** parka
capote/impermeable	**12** raincoat	anteojos/lentes/gafas de sol	**26** sunglasses
sombrero impermeable	**13** rain hat	orejeras	**27** ear muffs
gabardina/trinchera/impermeable	**14** trench coat	chaleco de plumas de ganso/acolchonado/acojinado	**28** down vest

A. What's the weather like today?
B. It's cool/cold/raining/snowing.
A. I think I'll wear my _____.

[1–6, 8–17, 19, 20, 22, 23, 25, 28]
A. May I help you?
B. Yes, please. I'm looking for a/an _____.

[7, 18, 21, 24, 26, 27]
A. May I help you?
B. Yes, please. I'm looking for _____.

What do you wear outside when the weather is cool?/when it's raining?/when it's very cold?

ROPA DE DORMIR Y ROPA INTERIOR

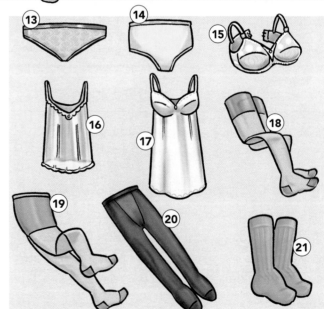

pijama/piyama	**1** pajamas
camisón	**2** nightgown
camisa de dormir	**3** nightshirt
bata de baño/albornoz	**4** bathrobe
zapatillas/babuchas/ pantuflas/chinelas	**5** slippers
mameluco/pelele/ pijamita de una pieza	**6** blanket sleeper
camiseta	**7** undershirt
calzoncillos/trusas	**8** underpants
calzoncillos bóxer/largos	**9** boxer shorts
suspensorios	**10** athletic supporter/ jockstrap
calzones largos/térmicos	**11** long underwear

medias/tobilleras/ calcetines/calcetas	**12** socks
panty bikini/pantaleta bikini	**13** panties
panty/pantaleta/calzonario/ braga/bombacha	**14** briefs/ underpants
sostenedor/sostén/ brassiere/bra	**15** bra
camisola/justillo	**16** camisole
peticote/fondo entero/ enagua/combinación	**17** slip
medias	**18** stockings
pantimedias	**19** pantyhose
leotardos/mallas	**20** tights
calcetines/medias/tobilleras/ tobimedias largas	**21** knee socks

A. I can't find my new _____.
B. Did you look in the bureau/dresser/closet?
A. Yes, I did.
B. Then it's/they're probably in the wash.

What sleepwear items do you wear? What sleepwear items do people in your family wear?

camiseta sin mangas	**1** tank top	leotardos	**12** leotard
pantalones/calzones cortos/ pantaloncillos/shorts	**2** running shorts	zapatos	**13** shoes
		zapatos de tacón alto	**14** (high) heels
vincha/bandana	**3** sweatband	zapatillas deportivas/tenis	**15** sneakers
traje deportivo/para correr/ chándal	**4** jogging suit		
		zapatillas para jugar tenis	**16** tennis shoes
camiseta/playera	**5** T-shirt	zapatillas para correr	**17** running shoes
pantalones cortos/calzones/ pantaloncillos de Lycra/malla	**6** lycra shorts/ bike shorts	zapatillas de botín alto/ medio botín/tenis altos	**18** high-tops/ high-top sneakers
sudadera	**7** sweatshirt	sandalias	**19** sandals
pantalones de sudadera	**8** sweatpants	chancletas/chinelas/ pantuflas	**20** thongs/flip-flops
batín	**9** cover-up		
vestido/traje de baño/ bañador	**10** swimsuit/ bathing suit	botas	**21** boots
		botas de trabajo	**22** work boots
traje de baño/bañador	**11** swimming trunks/ swimsuit/bathing suit		

[1–12]

A. Excuse me. I found this/these _____ in the dryer. Is it/Are they yours?

B. Yes. It's/They're mine. Thank you.

[13–22]

A. Are those new _____?

B. Yes, they are.

A. They're very nice.

B. Thanks.

Do you exercise? What do you do? What kind of clothing do you wear when you exercise?

What kind of shoes do you wear when you go to work or to school? when you exercise? when you relax at home? when you go out with friends or family members?

JEWELRY AND ACCESSORIES

JOYERÍA Y ACCESORIOS DE VESTIR

anillo/sortija	**1** ring		reloj/reloj de pulsera	**15** watch
anillo de compromiso	**2** engagement ring		pañuelo	**16** handkerchief
anillo de matrimonio	**3** wedding ring/ wedding band		llavero	**17** key ring
			monedero	**18** change purse
aretes/pendientes/pantallas	**4** earrings		billetera/cartera	**19** wallet
collar	**5** necklace		cinturón/correa	**20** belt
collar de perlas/ perlas	**6** pearl necklace/ pearls		bolso/bolsa/cartera	**21** purse/handbag/ pocketbook
cadena	**7** chain		carriel/bolsa de correa	**22** shoulder bag
collar de cuentas	**8** beads		maleta para libros/ mochila	**23** book bag
prendedor/broche	**9** pin			
dije/colgante/relicario	**10** locket		mochila/mochila de excursión	**24** backpack
pulsera/brazalete	**11** bracelet			
pasador/hebilla de cabello	**12** barrette		bolsa para maquillaje/ necessaire	**25** makeup bag
gemelos/mancuernas/yuntas	**13** cuff links			
tirantes	**14** suspenders		portafolios/maletín	**26** briefcase

A. Oh, no! I think I lost my **ring**!
B. I'll help you look for it.

A. Oh, no! I think I lost my **earrings**!
B. I'll help you look for them.

[In a store]
A. Excuse me. Is this/Are these _____ on sale this week?
B. Yes. It's/They're half price.

[On the street]
A. Help! Police! Stop that man/woman!
B. What happened?!
A. He/She just stole my _____ and my _____!

Do you like to wear jewelry? What jewelry do you have?

In your country, what do men, women, and children use to carry their things?

DESCRIBING CLOTHING

DESCRIPCIÓN DE LA ROPA

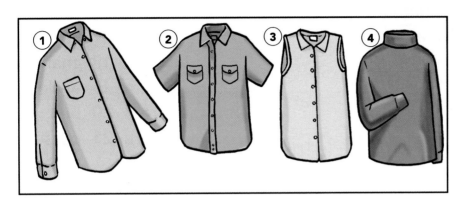

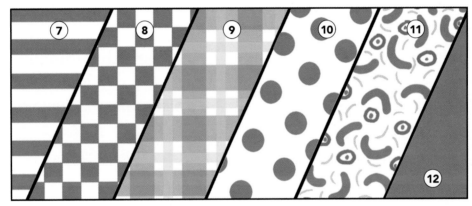

Tipos de ropa	Types of Clothing
camisa de mangas largas	**1** long-sleeved shirt
camisa de mangas cortas	**2** short-sleeved shirt
camisa sin mangas	**3** sleeveless shirt
camisa de cuello de tortuga/cisne	**4** turtleneck (shirt)
aretes	**5** pierced earrings
aretes de pinza/ de presión	**6** clip-on earrings

Patrones	Patterns
de rayas/de rayitas	**7** striped
de cuadros/de cuadritos	**8** checked
de diseño a cuadros escocés	**9** plaid
punteado(a) de bolas/bolitas (motitas)	**10** polka-dotted
estampado(a)	**11** print
azul sólido	**12** solid *blue*

Tallas/Tamaños	Sizes
petite/extra pequeño(a)	**13** extra-small
pequeño(a)	**14** small
mediano(a)	**15** medium
grande	**16** large
extra grande	**17** extra-large

[1–4]
A. May I help you?
B. Yes, please. I'm looking for a *shirt*.
A. What kind?
B. I'm looking for a *long-sleeved shirt*.

[7–12]
A. How do you like this _____ tie/shirt/skirt?
B. Actually, I prefer that _____ one.

[13–17]
A. What size are you looking for?
B. _____.

Describe your favorite clothing items. For each item, tell about the color, the size, and the pattern.

CLOTHING PROBLEMS AND ALTERATIONS

PROBLEMAS Y ARREGLOS DE LA ROPA

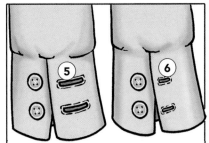

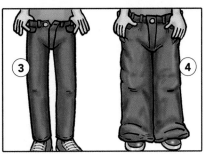

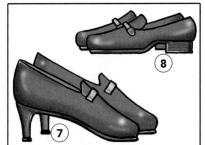

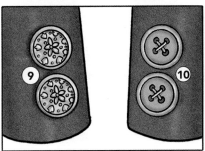

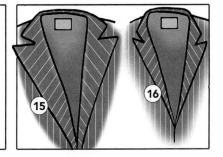

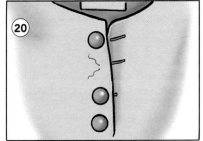

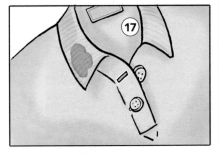

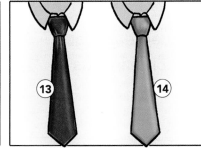

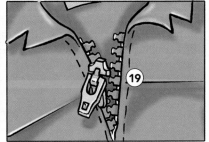

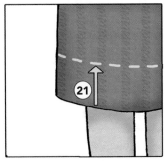

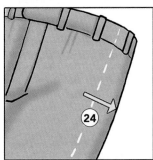

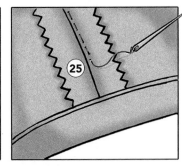

largo(a) – corto(a)	**1–2** long – short	*cuello* manchado	**17** stained *collar*
estrecho(a) – ancho(a)/flojo(a)	**3–4** tight – loose/baggy	*bolsillo* desgarrado/roto	**18** ripped/torn *pocket*
grande – chico(a)	**5–6** large/big – small	*cierre/cremallera* roto(a)	**19** broken *zipper*
alto(a) – bajo(a)	**7–8** high – low	le falta *un botón*	**20** missing *button*
elaborado(a) – sencillo(a)	**9–10** fancy – plain	subirle la basta/el dobladillo a *la falda*	**21** shorten the *skirt*
grueso(a)/pesado(a) – delgado(a)/liviano(a)	**11–12** heavy – light	alargar *las mangas*	**22** lengthen the *sleeves*
		meterle a la costura de *la chaqueta*	**23** take in the *jacket*
oscuro(a) – claro(a)	**13–14** dark – light	sacarle a la costura de *los pantalones*	**24** let out the *pants*
ancho(a) – angosto(a)	**15–16** wide – narrow	remendar *la costura*	**25** fix/repair the *seam*

[1–2]
A. Are the sleeves too **long**?
B. No. They're too **short**.

1–2	Are the sleeves too _____?	9–10	Are the buttons too _____?
3–4	Are the pants too _____?	11–12	Is the coat too _____?
5–6	Are the buttonholes too _____?	13–14	Is the color too _____?
7–8	Are the heels too _____?	15–16	Are the lapels too _____?

[17–20]
A. What's the matter with it?
B. It has a **stained** collar.

[21–25]
A. Please **shorten** the *skirt*.
B. **Shorten** the *skirt*? Okay.

Tell about the differences between clothing people wear now and clothing people wore a long time ago.

THE DEPARTMENT STORE

EL ALMACÉN/LA TIENDA DE DEPARTAMENTOS

guía/directorio	**1** (store) directory	Sección de artículos para el hogar/de cocina	**10** Housewares Department
Joyería	**2** Jewelry Counter	Sección de muebles	**11** Furniture Department
Perfumería	**3** Perfume Counter	Sección de electrodomésticos	**12** Household Appliances Department
escalera eléctrica/ automática/mecánica	**4** escalator	Sección de electrónica/ aparatos electrónicos	**13** Electronics Department
ascensor/elevador	**5** elevator	Mostrador de servicio al cliente	**14** Customer Service Counter
Sección de ropa de caballero	**6** Men's Clothing Department	servicios/baños para caballeros	**15** men's room
área de entrega de mercancía	**7** customer pickup area	servicios/baños para damas	**16** ladies' room
Sección de ropa de damas	**8** Women's Clothing Department	fuente/bebedero	**17** water fountain
Sección de ropa de niños	**9** Children's Clothing Department	cafetería/refresquería	**18** snack bar
		Mostrador para envolver regalos	**19** Gift Wrap Counter

A. Excuse me. Where's the **store directory**?
B. It's over there, next to the **Jewelry Counter**.
A. Thanks.
B. You're welcome.

A. Excuse me. Do you sell *ties**?
B. Yes. You can find *ties** in the ___[6, 8–13]___ /at the ___[2, 3]___ .
A. Thank you.

**ties/bracelets/dresses/toasters/. . .*

Describe a department store you know. Tell what is on each floor.

DE COMPRAS

comprar	**A** buy		etiqueta con el precio	**3** price tag
devolver	**B** return		recibo	**4** receipt
cambiar	**C** exchange		descuento/rebaja	**5** discount
probarse/ponerse	**D** try on		talla/tamaño	**6** size
pagar	**E** pay for		material	**7** material
obtener	**F** get some		cuidado de la ropa	**8** care instructions
información	information about		precio normal/regular	**9** regular price
			precio de descuento	**10** sale price
letrero para	**1** sale sign		precio	**11** price
anuncio de ofertas/			impuesto de ventas	**12** sales tax
descuentos/rebajas			precio total	**13** total price
etiqueta	**2** label			

A. May I help you?
B. Yes, please. I want to ___[A–F]___ this item.
A. Certainly. I'll be glad to help you.

A. ⎰ What's the ___[5–7, 9–13]___ ?
   ⎱ What are the ___[8]___ ?
B. _____.
A. Are you sure?
B. Yes. Look at the ___[1–4]___ !

Which stores in your area have sales? How often?

Tell about something you bought on sale.

VIDEO, AUDIO, TELÉFONOS Y CÁMARAS

televisor/televisión	**1** TV/television	equipo estereofónico portátil	**17** portable stereo system/boombox
DVD/disco de video digital	**2** DVD	reproductor de CD portátil	**18** personal CD player
reproductor de video digital/DVD	**3** DVD player	tocacintas/tocacasetes portátil	**19** personal cassette player
video/videocasete/videocinta	**4** video/videotape	audífonos/auriculares	**20** headphones
videocasetera/videograbadora/videoreproductora	**5** VCR	lector de MP3/reproductor de audio digital portátil	**21** personal digital audio player
videocámara/cámara de video	**6** camcorder/video camera	sistema de videojuego	**22** video game system
radio	**7** radio	videojuego/cartucho/paquete de videojuego	**23** video game
radio reloj despertador	**8** clock radio	teléfono	**24** telephone/phone
grabadora/magnetófono	**9** tape recorder	teléfono celular/móvil	**25** cell phone
micrófono	**10** microphone	contestadora automática	**26** answering machine
equipo estereofónico/de estereofonía/de estéreo	**11** stereo system/sound system	calculadora	**27** calculator
CD/disco compacto	**12** CD	cámara de 35 milímetros	**28** (35 millimeter) camera
reproductor de CD/discos compactos	**13** CD player	lente	**29** lens
		rollo de película/film	**30** film
audiocinta/audiocasete	**14** audiotape	cámara digital	**31** digital camera
casetera	**15** tape deck	tarjeta de memoria	**32** memory disk
bocinas/altavoces/altoparlantes	**16** speakers	flash removible	**33** flash (attachment)

A. May I help you?
B. Yes, please. I'm looking for a **TV**.

With 16, 20, 30, use: I'm looking for _____.

A. Excuse me. Do you sell _____(s)?*
B. Yes. We have a large selection of _____s.

With 30, use: Do you sell _____?

A. I like your new _____. Where did you get it/them?
B. At ......(name of store)......

What equipment in this lesson do you have or want?

In your opinion, which brands of equipment are the best?

COMPUTERS

COMPUTADORAS/ORDENADORES

Hardware/Equipo/ Soporte físico	Computer Hardware		
computadora/ ordenador personal	**1** (desktop) computer	ratón fijo con pelota de barrido/trackball	**13** track ball
CPU/procesadora central/ disco duro/base	**2** CPU/central processing unit	módem	**14** modem
monitor/pantalla electrónica	**3** monitor/screen	protector de sobrevoltaje	**15** surge protector
lector de CD-ROM	**4** CD-ROM drive	impresora	**16** printer
disco CD-ROM	**5** CD-ROM	escáner	**17** scanner
unidad de disquete	**6** disk drive	cable	**18** cable
disquete	**7** (floppy) disk		
teclado	**8** keyboard	**Programa informático/ de computación**	**Computer Software**
ratón	**9** mouse	procesador de textos	**19** word-processing program
pantalla plana/de cristal líquido	**10** flat panel screen/ LCD screen	procesador de hoja de cálculo	**20** spreadsheet program
microcomputadora/ laptop/portátil	**11** notebook computer	programa informático educativo	**21** educational software program
palanca	**12** joystick	juego de computadora	**22** computer game

A. Can you recommend a good **computer**?
B. Yes. This **computer** here is excellent.

A. Is that a new _____?
B. Yes.
A. Where did you get it?
B. At ......(name of store)......

A. May I help you?
B. Yes, please. Do you sell _____s?
A. Yes. We carry a complete line of _____s.

Do you use a computer? When?

In your opinion, why are computers important?

hacer un depósito	**A**	make a deposit
sacar dinero/ hacer un retiro	**B**	make a withdrawal
cambiar/cobrar un cheque	**C**	cash a check
comprar cheques de viajero	**D**	get traveler's checks
abrir una cuenta	**E**	open an account
pedir un préstamo	**F**	apply for a loan
cambiar divisas/ dinero/efectivo	**G**	exchange currency
ficha de depósito	**1**	deposit slip
ficha de retiro	**2**	withdrawal slip
cheque	**3**	check

cheque de viajero	**4**	traveler's check
libreta de banco	**5**	bankbook
tarjeta para cajero automático	**6**	ATM card
tarjeta de crédito	**7**	credit card
caja/caja fuerte/ de caudales	**8**	(bank) vault
caja de seguridad	**9**	safe deposit box
cajero(a)	**10**	teller
guardia de seguridad	**11**	security guard
cajero automático	**12**	ATM (machine)/ cash machine
funcionario(a) de banco	**13**	bank officer

[A–G]
A. Where are you going?
B. I'm going to the bank.
   I have to _____.

[5–7]
A. What are you looking for?
B. My _____. I can't find it
   anywhere!

[8–13]
A. How many _____s does the
   State Street Bank have?
B. ....

Do you have a bank account? What kind? Where? What do you do at the bank?

Do you ever use traveler's checks? When?

Do you have a credit card? What kind? When do you use it?

FINANZAS

(1)

(2) JOSE RIVERA
TO PALODINO AVENUE
SAN JOSE, CA 98215
396
PAY TO THE
ORDER OF
DATE
$
STATE
STREET BANK
DOLLARS
211365652: 230564 0396

(3)
5109 6231 3521 1721
2005 11/08
JOSE RIVERA

(4) 193560
$162.93
Pay to the Order of

(5)

(6) Lincoln Towers

(7) HOME FINANCE COMPANY

(8) City Power

(9) Western Bell

(10) G-STAR Energy

(11) Frank's Fuel Service

(12) WATER DEPARTMENT

(13) CableCorp

(14) Auto Finance

(15) MAXI Card

(16)

(17) 1096

(18)

(19)

(20) WATER DEPT. 46
Nov. Bill
DEPOSIT 945
Transfer
MAXI CARD 126
Total Balance Due
WESTERN BELL 64

(21) First National Bank
JANUARY

(22)

(23)

(24) WITHDRAWAL
DEPOSIT
TRANSFER

(25)

(26)

(27) KING TO SAVINGS
120.00

(28)

(29)

Formas de pago	Forms of Payment
dinero en efectivo/efectivo	**1** cash
cheque	**2** check
tarjeta de crédito	**3** credit card
orden de pago/giro	**4** money order
cheque de viajero	**5** traveler's check

Cuentas del hogar	Household Bills
renta/arriendo/alquiler	**6** rent
hipoteca	**7** mortgage payment
cuenta de la electricidad	**8** electric bill
cuenta del teléfono	**9** telephone bill
cuenta del gas	**10** gas bill
cuenta de la calefacción	**11** oil bill/ heating bill
cuenta del agua	**12** water bill
cuenta de la televisión por cable	**13** cable TV bill
pago del automóvil	**14** car payment
cuenta de la tarjeta de crédito	**15** credit card bill

Finanzas familiares	Family Finances
reconciliar la cuenta de cheques	**16** balance the checkbook
hacer/escribir un cheque	**17** write a check
hacer banca en línea/ banco virtual	**18** bank online
chequera/talonario de cheques	**19** checkbook
registro de cheques	**20** check register
estado de cuenta mensual	**21** monthly statement

Uso del cajero automático	Using an ATM Machine
inserte la tarjeta de cajero automático	**22** insert the ATM card
ingrese/teclee su número de identificación personal*	**23** enter your PIN* number
elija la transacción que desee realizar	**24** select a transaction
haga su depósito	**25** make a deposit
retire el dinero	**26** withdraw/get cash
transfiera fondos	**27** transfer funds
retire su tarjeta	**28** remove your card
retire el comprobante/recibo/ resguardo de la transacción	**29** take your receipt

* número de identificación personal/PIN   * personal identification number

A. Can I pay by ___[1, 2]___ / with a ___[3–5]___ ?
B. Yes, you can.

A. What are you doing?
B. { I'm paying the ___[6–15]___ .
    { I'm ___[16–18]___ ing.

A. What are you doing?
B. I'm looking for the ___[19–21]___ .

A. What should I do?
B. ___[22–29]___ .

What household bills do you receive? How much do you pay for the different bills?

Who takes care of the finances in your household? What does that person do?

Do you use ATM machines? If you do, how do you use them?

THE POST OFFICE

LA OFICINA DE CORREOS

carta	**1**	letter	formulario para registro en el servicio militar	**16** selective service registration form
tarjeta postal	**2**	postcard	formulario para solicitar pasaporte	**17** passport application form
aerograma	**3**	air letter	sobre	**18** envelope
paquete	**4**	package	remitente	**19** return address
primera clase	**5**	first class	destinatario	**20** mailing address
urgente	**6**	priority mail	código/área postal	**21** zip code
entrega inmediata/expreso	**7**	express mail	sello postal/estampilla/timbre	**22** stamp
paquete postal/encomienda	**8**	parcel post	buzón	**23** mail slot
correo certificado	**9**	certified mail	empleado(a) de correos	**24** postal worker/ postal clerk
sello postal/ estampilla/timbre	**10**	stamp	báscula	**25** scale
pliego de sellos/estampillas	**11**	sheet of stamps	máquina de estampillas	**26** stamp machine
rollo de sellos/estampillas	**12**	roll of stamps	cartero(a)	**27** letter carrier/ mail carrier
libreta de sellos/estampillas	**13**	book of stamps	camión de correos	**28** mail truck
giro/giro postal/telegráfico	**14**	money order	buzón	**29** mailbox
formulario de cambio de domicilio	**15**	change-of-address form		

[1–4]
A. Where are you going?
B. To the post office. I have to mail a/an _____.

[5–9]
A. How do you want to send it?
B. _____, please.

[10–17]
A. Next!
B. I'd like a _____, please.
A. Here you are.

[19–22]
A. Do you want me to mail this letter?
B. Yes, thanks.
A. Oops! You forgot the _____!

How often do you go to the post office? What do you do there?   Tell about the postal system in your country.

THE LIBRARY

LA BIBLIOTECA

BOOK 1 of 10 Entries
TITLE: Cat's pajamas
AUTHOR: Bradbury, Ray
CALL NUMBER: 841.238
STATUS: Checked out

Public Library

Amy L. Jackson

catálogo en línea	**1** online catalog
catálogo/tarjetero/fichero	**2** card catalog
carnet/tarjeta de identificación	**3** library card
fotocopiadora	**4** copier
estantes/librero/librería	**5** shelves
sección infantil	**6** children's section
libros infantiles	**7** children's books
sección de publicaciones periódicas/ revistas académicas	**8** periodical section
revistas	**9** magazines
periódicos	**10** newspapers
sección audiovisual	**11** media section
libros grabados/hablantes	**12** books on tape
audiocintas/audiocasetes	**13** audiotapes
CD/discos compactos	**14** CDs
videocintas	**15** videotapes

programa de computadora/ informático	**16** (computer) software
disco de video digital/DVD	**17** DVDs
sección de lenguas/ idomas extranjeros(as)	**18** foreign language section
libros en lenguas/ idiomas extranjeros(as)	**19** foreign language books
sección de referencia/consulta	**20** reference section
lector de microfilm	**21** microfilm reader
diccionario	**22** dictionary
enciclopedia	**23** encyclopedia
atlas	**24** atlas
mostrador de la sección de consultas	**25** reference desk
bibliotecario(a) de la sección de consulta	**26** (reference) librarian
mostrador de préstamos	**27** checkout desk
empleado(a) de biblioteca	**28** library clerk

[1, 2, 4–28]
A. Excuse me. Where's/Where are the _____?
B. Over there.

[22–24]
A. Excuse me. Where can I find a/an _____?
B. Look in the reference section.
A. Thank you.

[6–12, 17–20]
A. Can you help me? I'm looking for [7, 9, 10, 12, 17, 19] .
B. Look in the [6, 8, 11, 18, 20] over there.
A. Thanks.

Do you go to a library? Where? What does this library have?

Tell about how you use the library.

COMMUNITY INSTITUTIONS

INSTITUCIONES COMUNITARIAS

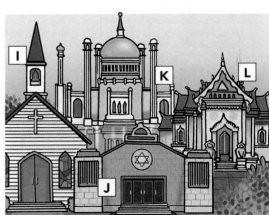

comisaría/estación/cuartel de policía	**A** police station	bombero(a)	**5** firefighter
cuartel/estación de bomberos	**B** fire station	sala de emergencias	**6** emergency room
hospital/sanatorio	**C** hospital	paramédico	**7** EMT/paramedic
palacio de gobierno/ayuntamiento	**D** town hall/city hall	ambulancia	**8** ambulance
centro recreativo	**E** recreation center	alcalde/	**9** mayor/
basurero público	**F** dump	intendente municipal	city manager
guardería infantil	**G** child-care center	sala de reuniones	**10** meeting room
centro para personas mayores	**H** senior center	gimnasio	**11** gym
		director de actividades	**12** activities director
iglesia	**I** church	salón de juegos	**13** game room
sinagoga	**J** synagogue	piscina/pileta/alberca	**14** swimming pool
mezquita	**K** mosque	recogedor de basura	**15** sanitation worker
templo	**L** temple	centro de reciclaje/reutilización	**16** recycling center
		auxiliar de guardería infantil	**17** child-care worker
telefonista para	**1** emergency	guardian infantile	**18** nursery
llamadas de emergencia	operator	cuarto de juegos	**19** playroom
policía	**2** police officer	enfermero(a) geriátrico(a)/	**20** eldercare worker/
radiopatrulla/patrulla/coche de policía	**3** police car	especialista en adultos mayores	senior care worker
vehículo autobomba	**4** fire engine		

[A–L]
A. Where are you going?
B. I'm going to the _____.

[1, 2, 5, 7, 12, 15, 17, 20]
A. What do you do?
B. I'm a/an _____.

[3, 4, 8]
A. Do you hear a siren?
B. Yes. There's a/an _____ coming up behind us.

What community institutions are in your city or town? Where are they located?

Which community institutions do you use? When?

EL CUERPO HUMANO I

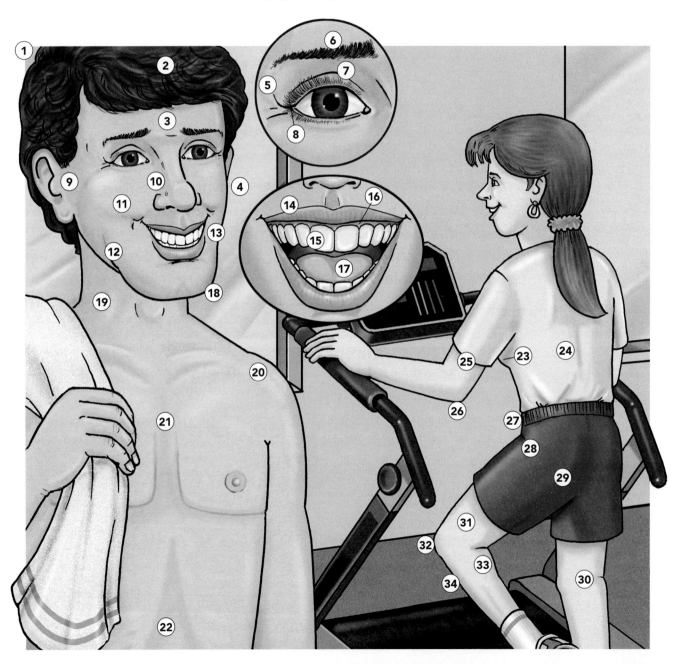

cabeza	**1** head	boca	**13** mouth	espalda	**24** back
cabello/pelo	**2** hair	labio	**14** lip	brazo	**25** arm
frente	**3** forehead	diente(s)	**15** tooth–teeth	codo	**26** elbow
cara	**4** face	encías	**16** gums	cintura	**27** waist
ojo	**5** eye	lengua	**17** tongue	cadera	**28** hip
ceja	**6** eyebrow	mentón/barbilla	**18** chin	nalgas	**29** buttocks
párpado	**7** eyelid	cuello	**19** neck	pierna	**30** leg
pestañas	**8** eyelashes	hombro	**20** shoulder	muslo	**31** thigh
oreja	**9** ear	pecho	**21** chest	rodilla	**32** knee
nariz	**10** nose	abdomen/vientre	**22** abdomen	pantorrilla	**33** calf
mejilla/pómulo	**11** cheek	seno/busto/	**23** breast	espinilla	**34** shin
mandíbula/	**12** jaw	pecho			
quijada					

A. My doctor checked my **head** and said everything is okay.
B. I'm glad to hear that.

[1, 3–7, 9–26, 28–34]
A. Ooh!
B. What's the matter?
  { My _____ hurts!
  { My _____s hurt!

A. Doctor's Office.
B. Hello. This is ....._(name)_..... .
   I'm concerned about my _____.
A. Do you want to make an appointment?
B. Yes, please.

Describe yourself as completely as you can.

EL CUERPO HUMANO II

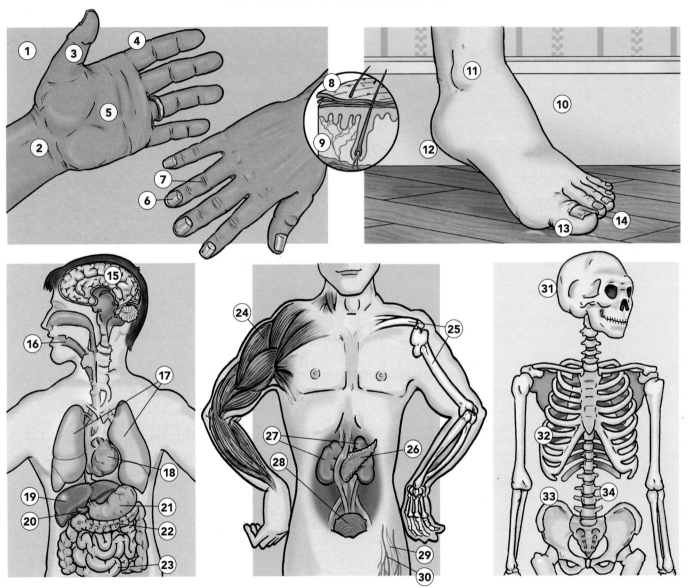

mano	**1**	hand	dedo del pie	**13**	toe	huesos	**25**	bones

mano · **1** hand
muñeca · **2** wrist
pulgar · **3** thumb
dedo · **4** finger
palma · **5** palm
uña · **6** fingernail
nudillo · **7** knuckle
piel · **8** skin
nervio · **9** nerve
pie · **10** foot
tobillo · **11** ankle
talón · **12** heel

dedo del pie · **13** toe
uña del dedo del pie · **14** toenail
cerebro · **15** brain
garganta · **16** throat
pulmones · **17** lungs
corazón · **18** heart
hígado · **19** liver
vesícula biliar · **20** gallbladder
estómago · **21** stomach
intestino grueso · **22** large intestine
intestino delgado · **23** small intestine
músculos · **24** muscles

huesos · **25** bones
páncreas · **26** pancreas
riñones · **27** kidneys
vejiga · **28** bladder
venas · **29** veins
arterias · **30** arteries
cráneo · **31** skull
caja torácica · **32** ribcage
pelvis · **33** pelvis
columna vertebral/espina dorsal · **34** spinal column/spinal cord

[1–7, 10–14]
A. What's the matter?
B. I hurt my **hand**.

[1–14]
A. Does your **wrist** hurt when I do THIS?
B. Yes, it does.

[8, 15–34]
A. How am I, Doctor?
B. Well, I'm a little concerned about your **skin**.

Which parts of the body on pages 162–165 are most important at school? at work? when you play your favorite sport?

AILMENTS, SYMPTOMS, AND INJURIES I

MALESTARES, SÍNTOMAS Y LESIONES I

  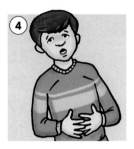  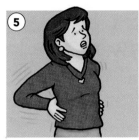 

  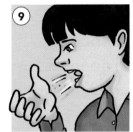   

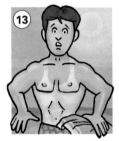   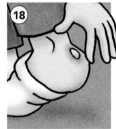 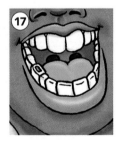 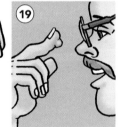

dolor de cabeza	**1** headache		torticolis	**14** stiff neck
dolor de oído	**2** earache		moquear	**15** runny nose
dolor de muelas/dientes	**3** toothache		hemorragia nasal	**16** bloody nose
dolor de estómago	**4** stomachache		caries	**17** cavity
dolor de espalda	**5** backache		ampolla	**18** blister
dolor de garganta	**6** sore throat		verruga	**19** wart
fiebre/calentura	**7** fever/temperature		hipo	**20** (the) hiccups
catarro/resfriado	**8** cold		escalofrío	**21** (the) chills
tos	**9** cough		calambre/retortijón	**22** cramps
infección	**10** infection		diarrea	**23** diarrhea
sarpullido/salpullido	**11** rash		dolor en el pecho	**24** chest pain
picadura/picada	**12** insect bite		jadeo	**25** shortness of breath
quemadura de sol	**13** sunburn		laringitis	**26** laryngitis

A. What's the matter?
B. I have a/an ___[1–19]___ .

A. What's the matter?
B. I have ___[20–26]___ .

A. How do you feel?
B. Not so good.
A. What's the matter?
B. ....
A. I'm sorry to hear that.

A. Are you okay?
B. Not really. I don't feel very well.
A. What's wrong?
B. ....
A. I'm sorry to hear that.

Tell about a time you had one of these problems.

What do you do when you have a cold? a stomachache? an insect bite? the hiccups?

MALESTARES, SÍNTOMAS Y LESIONES II

desmayo	**1** faint		torcerse (el pie)	**13** twist
(tener) mareo	**2** dizzy		arañazo	**14** scratch
tener náuseas	**3** nauseous		raspadura/rasguño	**15** scrape
hinchazón del abdomen/gases	**4** bloated		moretón/magulladura/cardenal	**16** bruise
estar congestionado(a)	**5** congested		quemadura	**17** burn
estar agotado(a)	**6** exhausted		lesionarse	**18** hurt–hurt
toser	**7** cough		cortarse	**19** cut–cut
estornudar	**8** sneeze		(tener) en esguince	**20** sprain
respiración sibilante	**9** wheeze		dislocación	**21** dislocate
eructar	**10** burp		fracturarse	**22** break–broke
vomitar	**11** vomit / throw up		hinchazón	**23** swollen
sangrar	**12** bleed		comezón/picazón	**24** itchy

A. What's the problem?

B. { I feel ____ [1–4] ____ .
I'm ____ [5, 6] ____ .

A. Can you describe your symptoms?

B. I'm ____ [7–12] ____ ing a lot.

A. What happened?

B. { I ____ [13–19] ____ ed my ....
I think I ____ [20–22] ____ ed my ....
My .... is/are ____ [23, 24] ____ .

Tell about the last time you didn't feel well.
What was the matter?

Tell about a time you hurt yourself. What happened?
How? What did you do about it?

FIRST AID

PRIMEROS AUXILIOS

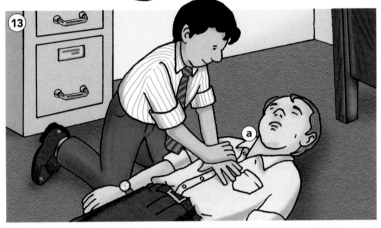

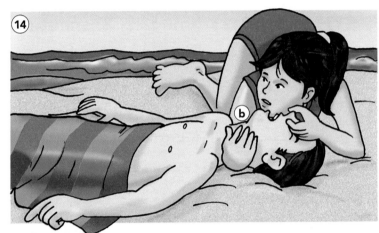

Spanish	#	English
manual de primeros auxilios	1	first-aid manual
maletín/botiquín de primeros auxilios	2	first-aid kit
tirita/curita	3	bandage/Band-Aid™
almohadilla estéril	4	sterile (dressing) pad
agua oxigenada	5	hydrogen peroxide
ungüento antibiótico	6	antibiotic ointment
gasa	7	gauze
esparadrapo/cinta adhesiva	8	adhesive tape
pinzas	9	tweezers
venda elástica	10	elastic bandage/Ace™ bandage
aspirina	11	aspirin
analgésico sin aspirina	12	non-aspirin pain reliever

Spanish	#	English
RCP*	13	CPR*
no tiene pulso	a	has no pulse
respiración artificial/asistida	14	rescue breathing
no está respirando	b	isn't breathing
la maniobra de Heimlich	15	the Heimlich maneuver
está atorado/se está asfixiando	c	is choking
entablillar	16	splint
se rompió un dedo	d	broke a finger
torniquete	17	tourniquet
está sangrando	e	is bleeding

* respiración artificial/resucitación cardiopulmonar   * cardiopulmonary resuscitation

A. Do we have any ___[3, 4, 10]___s/___[5–9, 11, 12]___?
B. Yes. Look in the first-aid kit.

A. Help! My friend ___[a-e]___!
B. I can help!
{ I know how to do ___[13-15]___.
{ I can make a ___[16, 17]___.

Do you have a first-aid kit? If you do, what's in it? If you don't, where can you buy one?

Tell about a time when you gave or received first aid.

Where can a person learn first aid in your community?

MEDICAL EMERGENCIES AND ILLNESSES

EMERGENCIAS MÉDICAS Y ENFERMEDADES/DOLENCIAS

herido(a)/lastimado(a)	**1** hurt/injured	infección (de estreptococos) en la garganta	**14** strep throat
en estado de choque	**2** in shock	sarampión	**15** measles
inconsciente	**3** unconscious	paperas	**16** mumps
insolación	**4** heatstroke	varicela/viruela loca	**17** chicken pox
congelado(a)/daño en el cuerpo por el frío	**5** frostbite	asma	**18** asthma
ataque al corazón	**6** heart attack	cáncer	**19** cancer
reacción alérgica	**7** allergic reaction	depresión	**20** depression
tragar veneno	**8** swallow poison	diabetes	**21** diabetes
sobredosis de medicinas/drogas	**9** overdose on drugs	afección del corazón	**22** heart disease
caerse	**10** fall–fell	presión alta/hipertensión	**23** high blood pressure/ hypertension
sufrir un choque eléctrico	**11** get–got an electric shock	tuberculosis	**24** TB/tuberculosis
influenza/gripe	**12** the flu/influenza	SIDA*	**25** AIDS*
infección de oído	**13** an ear infection		

* Síndrome de Inmunodeficiencia Adquirida

* Acquired Immune Deficiency Syndrome

A. What's the matter?

B. My .... { is _[1–3]_ . / has _[4, 5]_ . / is having a/an _[6, 7]_ .

A. What's your address?

B. _(address)_ .

A. What happened?

B. My .... _[8–11]_ ed.

A. What's your location?

B. _(address)_ in _(city/town)_ .

A. My .... is sick.

B. What's the matter?

A. He/She has _[12–25]_ .

B. I'm sorry to hear that.

Tell about a medical emergency that happened to you or someone you know.

Which illnesses in this lesson are you familiar with?

THE MEDICAL EXAM

EL EXAMEN MÉDICO

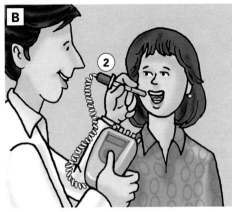

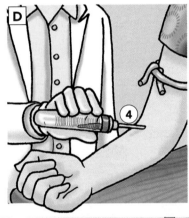

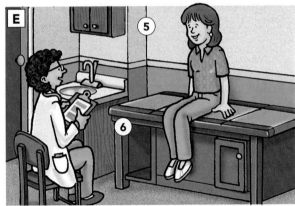

medir*le* y pesarle **A** measure *your* height and weight

tomar*le* la temperatura **B** take *your* temperature

tomar*le* la presión arterial **C** check *your* blood pressure

sacar*le* sangre **D** draw some blood

hacer*le* algunas preguntas sobre *su* salud **E** ask *you* some questions about *your* health

examinar*le* los ojos, oídos, nariz y garganta **F** examine *your* eyes, ears, nose, and throat

escuchar*le* el corazón **G** listen to *your* heart

tomarle una radiografía del pecho **H** take a chest X-ray

balanza/báscula **1** scale

termómetro **2** thermometer

manómetro **3** blood pressure gauge

aguja/jeringa/jeringuilla **4** needle

consultorio **5** examination room

camilla de examen/mesa de reconocimiento **6** examination table

cartilla para medir la vista **7** eye chart

estetoscopio **8** stethoscope

máquina de rayos X/ radiografías **9** X-ray machine

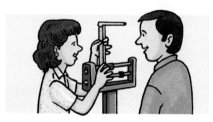

[A–H]
A. Now I'm going to **measure your height and weight**.
B. All right.

[A–H]
A. What did the doctor/nurse do during the examination?
B. She/He **measured my height and weight**.

[1–3, 5–9]
A. So, how do you like our new **scale?**
B. It's very nice, doctor.

How often do you have a medical exam?

What does the doctor/nurse do?

MEDICAL AND DENTAL PROCEDURES

PROCEDIMIENTOS MÉDICOS Y DENTALES

limpiar la herida	**A** clean the wound	formulario para la historia/el historial clínico(a)	**4** medical history form
coser/suturar la herida	**B** close the wound	consultorio	**5** examination room
vendar la herida	**C** dress the wound	médico(a)/doctor(a)	**6** doctor/ physician
limpiarle los dientes	**D** clean *your* teeth	paciente	**7** patient
examinarle los dientes	**E** examine *your* teeth	enfermero(a)	**8** nurse
ponerle una inyección con anestesia/ Novocaína™	**F** give *you* a shot of anesthetic/ Novocaine™	motas/bolas de algodón	**9** cotton balls
taladrar el diente/ la caries	**G** drill the cavity	alcohol	**10** alcohol
rellenar la cavidad/ el diente	**H** fill the tooth	sutura/puntos	**11** stitches

bolsa de hielo	**16** ice pack		
receta médica	**17** prescription		
cabestrillo	**18** sling		
yeso/enyesado/ escayola	**19** cast		
férula/ entablillado	**20** brace		
higienista	**21** hygienist		
mascarilla/ máscara	**22** mask		
guantes	**23** gloves		
dentista	**24** dentist		
asistente (del dentista)	**25** dental assistant		
fresa/taladro	**26** drill		
empaste/ relleno	**27** filling		

sala de espera **1** waiting room
recepcionista **2** receptionist
tarjeta de seguro médico **3** insurance card

gasa **12** gauze
esparadrapo **13** tape
inyección **14** injection/shot
muletas **15** crutches

A. Now I'm going to _____[A–H]____.
B. Will it hurt?
A. Just a little.

A. I'm going to { give you (a/an) __[14–17]__.
{ put your .... in a __[18–20]__.
B. Okay.

A. I need { __[9, 10, 12, 13, 23]__.
{ a __[22, 26]__.
B. Here you are.

Tell about a personal experience you had with a medical or dental procedure.

MEDICAL ADVICE

RECOMENDACIONES MÉDICAS

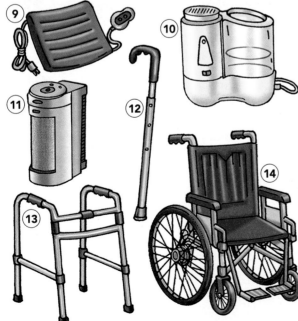

guardar cama	**1**	rest in bed	bastón	**12**	cane
tomar líquidos	**2**	drink fluids	andadera	**13**	walker
hacer gárgaras	**3**	gargle	silla de ruedas	**14**	wheelchair
ponerse a dieta	**4**	go on a diet	análisis/pruebas de sangre	**15**	blood work / blood tests
hacer ejercicio	**5**	exercise			
tomar vitaminas	**6**	take vitamins	exámenes médicos/ análisis	**16**	tests
ver a un especialista	**7**	see a specialist			
recibir tratamiento de acupuntura	**8**	get acupuncture	fisioterapia	**17**	physical therapy
bolsa caliente/almohadilla eléctrica	**9**	heating pad	operación/cirugía	**18**	surgery
humidificador	**10**	humidifier	consejo personal/terapia	**19**	counseling
purificador de aire	**11**	air purifier	frenos	**20**	braces

A. I think you should ___[1–8]___.
B. I understand.

A. I think { you should use a/an ___[9–14]___.
            { you need ___[15–20]___.
B. I see.

A. What did the doctor say?

B. The doctor thinks { I should ___[1–8]___.
                     { I should use a/an ___[9–14]___.
                     { I need ___[15–20]___.

Tell about medical advice a doctor gave you. What did the doctor say? Did you follow the advice?

REMEDIOS/MEDICINAS

aspirina	**1**	aspirin	gotas para los ojos	**10** eye drops
píldoras para el resfriado/catarro	**2**	cold tablets	ungüento/pomada	**11** ointment
			pomada/crema	**12** cream/creme
vitaminas	**3**	vitamins	loción	**13** lotion
jarabe para la tos	**4**	cough syrup	píldora	**14** pill
analgésico sin aspirina	**5**	non-aspirin pain reliever	tableta/pastilla	**15** tablet
			cápsula	**16** capsule
pastillas para la tos	**6**	cough drops	cápsula comprimida	**17** caplet
pastillas para la garganta	**7**	throat lozenges	cucharadita/ cuchara de té	**18** teaspoon
antiácido en tabletas	**8**	antacid tablets		
descongestionante nasal (en atomizador/spray)	**9**	decongestant spray/ nasal spray	cucharada/ cuchara sopera	**19** tablespoon

A. What did the doctor say?
B. She told me to take
   ___[1–4]___ /a ___[5]___.

A. What did the doctor recommend?
B. He told me to use
   ___[6–13]___.

[14–19]
A. What's the dosage?
B. One _____ every four hours.

What medicines in this lesson do you have at home? What other medicines do you have?

What do you take or use for a fever? a headache? a stomachache? a sore throat? a cold? a cough?

Tell about any medicines in your country that are different from the ones in this lesson.

THE HOSPITAL

EL HOSPITAL

cuarto del/ de la paciente	**A**	**patient's room**	estación de enfermeros(as)	**B**	**nurse's station**
paciente	**1**	patient	enfermero(a)	**12**	nurse
bata de hospital	**2**	hospital gown	especialista en dietética	**13**	dietitian
cama de hospital	**3**	hospital bed	asistente de enfermero(a)	**14**	orderly
control de la cama	**4**	bed control			
timbre	**5**	call button	sala de operaciones/ quirófano	**C**	**operating room**
venoclisis/ intravenosa	**6**	I.V.			
monitor/pantalla con control de signos vitales	**7**	vital signs monitor	cirujano(a)	**15**	surgeon
			enfermero(a) quirúrgico(a)	**16**	surgical nurse
mesa de cama	**8**	bed table	anestesiólogo(a)/ anestesista	**17**	anesthesiologist
cuña/paleta/bacín/ cómodo/silleta	**9**	bed pan			
cuadrícula/ hoja clínica	**10**	medical chart	sala de espera	**D**	**waiting room**
médico(a)/ doctor(a)	**11**	doctor/ physician	voluntario(a)	**18**	volunteer

sala de partos	**E**	**birthing room/ delivery room**
ginecólogo(a)/obstetra	**19**	obstetrician
enfermera comadrona/partera	**20**	midwife/ nurse-midwife
sala de emergencias	**F**	**emergency room/ER**
paramédico(a)	**21**	emergency medical technician/EMT
camilla	**22**	gurney
departamento de radiología	**G**	**radiology department**
técnico(a) radiólogo(a)	**23**	X-ray technician
radiólogo(a)	**24**	radiologist
laboratorio	**H**	**laboratory/lab**
técnico(a) de laboratorio	**25**	lab technician

A. This is your ___[2–10]___.
B. I see.

A. Do you work here?
B. Yes. I'm a/an ___[11–21, 23–25]___.

A. Where's the ___[11–21, 23–25]___?
B. She's/He's { in the ___[A, C–H]___.
                at the ___[B]___.

Tell about an experience you or a family member had in the hospital.

PERSONAL HYGIENE

HIGIENE PERSONAL

me estoy cepillando los dientes **A brush *my* teeth**
cepillo de dientes **1** toothbrush
pasta de dientes/crema dental **2** toothpaste

estoy usando el hilo dental **B floss *my* teeth**
seda/hilo dental/hilo de dientes **3** dental floss

estoy haciendo gárgaras — **C gargle**
antiséptico/enjuague bucal — **4** mouthwash

me estoy bañando en la tina — **D bathe/take a bath**
jabón — **5** soap
baño de burbujas/espuma — **6** bubble bath

me estoy bañando/duchando — **E take a shower**
gorra(o) de baño — **7** shower cap

me estoy lavando el pelo/cabello — **F wash *my* hair**
champú — **8** shampoo
acondicionador/enjuague — **9** conditioner

me estoy secando el pelo/cabello — **G dry *my* hair**
secador(a) de pelo/cabello — **10** hair dryer/blow dryer

me estoy peinando — **H comb *my* hair**
peine/peinilla — **11** comb

me estoy cepillando el pelo/cabello — **I brush *my* hair**
cepillo para el pelo/cabello — **12** brush

me estoy afeitando/rasurando — **J shave**
crema para afeitarse/rasurarse — **13** shaving cream

maquinilla de afeitar/rastrillo — **14** razor
máquina de afeitar eléctrica — **15** electric shaver

me estoy arreglando las uñas — **K do *my* nails**
lima de metal para las uñas — **16** nail file
cortaúñas — **17** nail clipper
tijeras — **18** scissors
esmalte de uñas/barniz — **19** nail polish

me estoy poniendo . . . — **L put on . . .**
desodorante — **20** deodorant
colonia/perfume — **21** cologne/perfume
talco/polvo — **22** powder
bloqueador solar/loción protectora — **23** sunscreen

me estoy maquillando — **M put on makeup**
colorete — **24** blush/rouge
delineador de ojos — **25** eyeliner
sombra para los ojos — **26** eye shadow
rímel/pintador de pestañas — **27** mascara
pintalabios/lápiz de labios/carmín/bilé — **28** lipstick

me estoy lustrando/limpiando los zapatos — **N polish *my* shoes**
betún/cera para zapatos — **29** shoe polish
cordones de zapatos/agujetas — **30** shoelaces

[A–K, L (20–23), M, N]
A. What are you doing?
B. I'm _____ing.

[1, 7, 10–12, 14–18, 30]
A. Excuse me. Where can I find _____(s)?
B. They're in the next aisle.

[2–6, 8, 9, 13, 19–29]
A. Excuse me. Where can I find _____?
B. It's in the next aisle.

Which of these personal care products do you use?

You're going on a trip. Make a list of the personal care products you need to take with you.

BABY CARE

EL CUIDADO DEL/DE LA BEBÉ

darle la comida	**A feed**
papillas/comidas de bebé en frasquitos o tarritos/colados	**1** baby food
babero	**2** bib
biberón/mamadera/tetero/mamila	**3** bottle
chupón/chupete/tetina/tetilla/mamadera	**4** nipple
fórmula/leche en polvo	**5** formula
vitaminas en líquido/gotas	**6** (liquid) vitamins
cambiarle el pañal	**B change the baby's diaper**
pañal desechable	**7** disposable diaper
pañal de tela/algodón	**8** cloth diaper
imperdible/alfiler de gancho/seguridad	**9** diaper pin
toallitas húmedas desechables	**10** (baby) wipes
polvo/talco para niños	**11** baby powder
pañal entrenador/pull up	**12** training pants
pomada/ungüento	**13** ointment

bañar	**C bathe**
champú para niños	**14** baby shampoo
palillo de algodón/hisopo	**15** cotton swab
loción para niños	**16** baby lotion
cargar	**D hold**
chupete/consuelo/chupón	**17** pacifier
chupador/chupón/mordedera	**18** teething ring
amamantar	**E nurse**
vestir	**F dress**
mecer/arrullar	**G rock**
guardería infantil	**19** child-care center
trabajador(a) de guardería infantil	**20** child-care worker
mecedora	**21** rocking chair
leerle a	**H read to**
armario	**22** cubby
jugar con	**I play with**
juguetes	**23** toys

A. What are you doing?

B. {
I'm ___[A, C–I]___ ing the baby.
I'm ___[B]___ ing.
}

A. Do we need anything from the store?

B. Yes. We need some more {
___[2–4, 7–9, 15, 17, 18]___ s.
___[1, 5, 6, 10–14, 16]___ .
}

In your opinion, which are better: cloth diapers or disposable diapers? Why?

Tell about baby products in your country.

SCHOOL SUBJECTS

CURSOS/MATERIAS

matemáticas	**1**	math/mathematics	español	**12** Spanish
inglés	**2**	English	francés	**13** French
historia	**3**	history	economía doméstica	**14** home economics
geografía	**4**	geography	artes industriales/taller	**15** industrial arts/shop
gobierno/civismo	**5**	government	comercio/negocios	**16** business education
ciencias	**6**	science	educación física	**17** physical education/ P.E.
biología	**7**	biology		
química	**8**	chemistry	curso para aprender a manejar/conducir	**18** driver's education/ driver's ed
física	**9**	physics		
salud/higiene	**10**	health	arte	**19** art
informática/ computación	**11**	computer science	música	**20** music

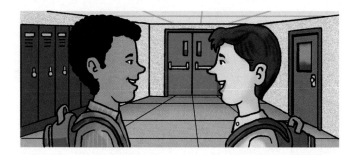

A. What do you have next period?
B. **Math**. How about you?
A. **English**.
B. There's the bell. I've got to go.

What is/was your favorite subject? Why?

In your opinion, what's the most interesting subject? the most difficult subject? Why do you think so?

EXTRACURRICULAR ACTIVITIES

ACTIVIDADES EXTRACURRICULARES

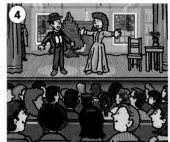

banda	**1**	band
orquesta	**2**	orchestra
coro	**3**	choir/chorus
drama/teatro	**4**	drama
fútbol americano	**5**	football
animadores(as)	**6**	cheerleading/ pep squad
asociación de estudiantes	**7**	student government
servicio comunitario	**8**	community service
periódico estudiantil	**9**	school newspaper
anuario	**10**	yearbook

revista literaria	**11**	literary magazine
equipo/cuadrilla de luces y sonido	**12**	A.V. crew
club de oratoria	**13**	debate club
club de informática/ computación	**14**	computer club
club de relaciones internacionales	**15**	international club
club de ajedrez	**16**	chess club

[1–6]
A. Are you going home right after school?
B. No. I have **band** practice.

[7–16]
A. What are you going to do after school today?
B. I have a **student government** meeting.

What extracurricular activities do/did you participate in?

Which extracurricular activities in this lesson are there in schools in your country? What other activities are there?

MATEMÁTICAS

Arithmetic   Aritmética

$$2+1=3 \qquad 8-3=5 \qquad 4\times2=8 \qquad 10\div2=5$$

addition	subtraction	multiplication	division
suma	resta	multiplicación	división

2 **plus** 1 **equals*** 3.   8 **minus** 3 **equals*** 5.   4 **times** 2 **equals*** 8.   10 **divided by** 2 **equals*** 5.

* *También se dice:* **is**

A. How much is *two plus one*?
B. *Two plus one* equals / is *three.*

Make conversations for the arithmetic problems above and others.

Fractions   Fracciones

one quarter / one fourth	one third	one half / half	two thirds	three quarters / three fourths

A. Is this on sale?
B. Yes. It's _____ off the regular price.

A. Is the gas tank almost empty?
B. It's about _____ full.

Percents   Porcentajes

10%
ten
percent

50%
fifty
percent

75%
seventy-five
percent

100%
one-hundred
percent

A. How did you do on the test?
B. I got _____ percent of the answers right.

A. What's the weather forecast?
B. There's a _____ percent chance of rain.

Types of Math   Tipos de matemáticas

$5y-5y+3=$

algebra
álgebra

geometry
geometría

$\sin(y)=x$

trigonometry
trigonometría

$\int_2^6 g(x)\,dx$

calculus
cálculo

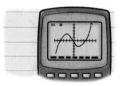

statistics
estadística

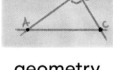

A. What math course are you taking this year?
B. I'm taking _____.

Are you good at math?

What math courses do/did you take in school?

Tell about something you bought on sale. How much off the regular price was it?

Research and discuss: What percentage of people in your country live in cities? live on farms? work in factories?

MEDIDAS Y FORMAS GEOMÉTRICAS

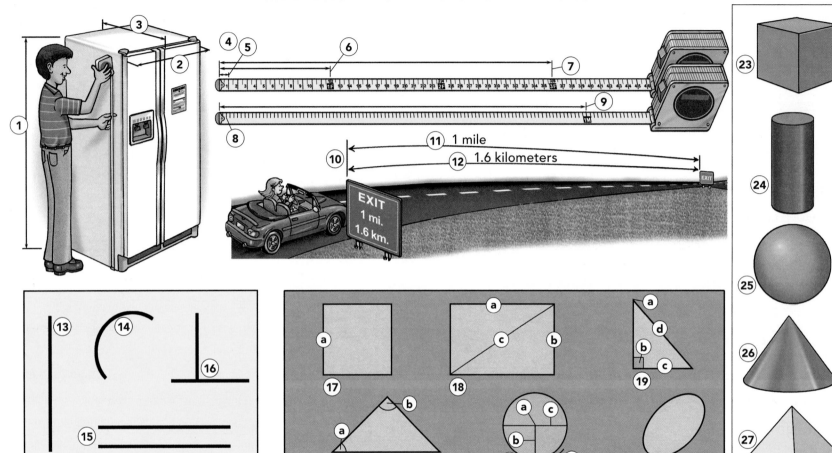

Medidas		Measurements		yarda	**7**	yard		Líneas		Lines
altura	**1**	height		centímetro	**8**	centimeter		línea recta	**13**	straight line
ancho/anchura	**2**	width		metro	**9**	meter		línea curva	**14**	curved line
profundidad	**3**	depth		distancia	**10**	distance		líneas paralelas	**15**	parallel lines
largo/longitud	**4**	length		milla	**11**	mile		líneas	**16**	perpendicular
pulgada	**5**	inch		kilómetro	**12**	kilometer		perpendiculares		lines
pie-pies	**6**	foot–feet								

Formas geométricas	Geometric Shapes
cuadrado	**17** square
lado	**a** side
rectángulo	**18** rectangle
largo	**a** length
altura	**b** width
diagonal	**c** diagonal
triángulo rectángulo	**19** right triangle
vértice	**a** apex
ángulo recto	**b** right angle
base	**c** base
hipotenusa	**d** hypotenuse
triángulo isósceles	**20** isosceles triangle
ángulo agudo	**a** acute angle
ángulo obtuso	**b** obtuse angle

círculo	**21** circle
centro	**a** center
radio	**b** radius
diámetro	**c** diameter
circunferencia	**d** circumference
elipse	**22** ellipse/oval

Sólidos/Figuras tridimensionales	Solid Figures
cubo	**23** cube
cilindro	**24** cylinder
esfera	**25** sphere
cono	**26** cone
pirámide	**27** pyramid

[1–9]
A. What's the ___[1–4]___?
B. .... ___[5–9]___(s).

[11–12]
A. What's the distance?
B. .... _____(s).

1 inch (1") = 2.54 centimeters (cm)
1 foot (1') = 0.305 meters (m)
1 yard (1 yd.) = 0.914 meters (m)
1 mile (mi.) = 1.6 kilometers (km)

[17–22]
A. What shape is this?
B. It's a/an _____.

[23–27]
A. What figure is this?
B. It's a/an _____.

[13–27]
A. This painting is magnificent!
B. Hmm. I don't think so. It just looks like a lot of _____s and _____s to me!

EL IDIOMA INGLÉS: LENGUAJE Y REDACCIÓN

Types of Sentences & Parts of Speech   Tipos de oraciones y elementos del habla

A *Students study in the new library.*
① ② ③ ④ ⑤

C *Read page nine.*

B *Do they study hard?*
⑥ ⑦

D *This cake is fantastic!*

declarativo	**A** declarative	sustantivo	**1** noun	adjetivo	**5** adjective
interrogativo	**B** interrogative	verbo	**2** verb	pronombre	**6** pronoun
imperativo	**C** imperative	preposición	**3** preposition	adverbio	**7** adverb
exclamativo	**D** exclamatory	artículo	**4** article		

A. What type of sentence is this?
B. It's a/an ___[A–D]___ sentence.

A. What part of speech is this?
B. It's a/an ___[1–7]___ .

Punctuation Marks & the Writing Process

Signos de puntuación y el proceso de la escritura

punto	**8** period	dos puntos	**14** colon	título	**a** title
signo de interrogación	**9** question mark	punto y coma	**15** semi-colon	párrafo	**b** paragraph
signo de exclamación	**10** exclamation point	recolectar y asociar ideas	**16** brainstorm ideas	corregir/revisar/editar	**19** make corrections/revise/edit
coma	**11** comma	organizar *mis* ideas	**17** organize *my* ideas	recibir reacciones/comentarios	**20** get feedback
apóstrofe	**12** apostrophe	escribir un borrador	**18** write a first draft	pasar en limpio/escribir la copia final	**21** write a final copy/rewrite
comillas	**13** quotation marks				

A. Did you find any mistakes?
B. Yes. You forgot to put a/an ___[8–15]___ in this sentence.

A. Are you working on your composition?
B. Yes. I'm ___[16–21]___ing.

LA LITERATURA Y LA ESCRITURA

ficción	**1** fiction		artículo periodístico	**11** newspaper article
novela	**2** novel		editorial	**12** editorial
cuento	**3** short story		carta	**13** letter
poesía/poemas	**4** poetry/poems		tarjeta postal	**14** postcard
no ficción	**5** non-fiction		nota	**15** note
biografía	**6** biography		invitación	**16** invitation
autobiografía	**7** autobiography		nota de agradecimiento	**17** thank-you note
ensayo	**8** essay		memorándum/memoranda	**18** memo
trabajo/reporte/ informe escolar	**9** report		mensaje por correo electrónico/e-mail	**19** e-mail
artículo de revista	**10** magazine article		mensaje instantáneo	**20** instant message

A. What are you doing?

B. I'm writing $\begin{cases} \underline{\quad [1, 4, 5] \quad}. \\ \text{a/an} \underline{\quad [2, 3, 6–20] \quad}. \end{cases}$

What kind of literature do you like to read? What are some of your favorite books? Who is your favorite author?

Do you like to read newspapers and magazines? Which ones do you read?

Do you sometimes send or receive letters, postcards, notes, e-mail, or instant messages? Tell about the people you communicate with, and how.

GEOGRAPHY

GEOGRAFÍA

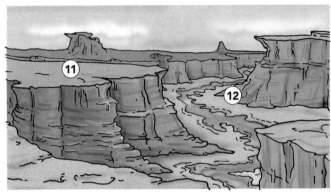

bosque	**1** forest/woods		desierto	**14** desert
colina	**2** hill		selva tropical/jungla	**15** jungle
cordillera/sierra	**3** mountain range		playa/costa	**16** seashore/shore
cumbre	**4** mountain peak		bahía	**17** bay
valle	**5** valley		océano	**18** ocean
lago	**6** lake		isla	**19** island
llanuras	**7** plains		península	**20** peninsula
pradera	**8** meadow		selva húmeda/	**21** rainforest
arroyo/quebrada/riachuelo	**9** stream/brook		tropical	
laguna/charca/estanque	**10** pond		río	**22** river
meseta	**11** plateau		cascada (pequeña)/	**23** waterfall
cañón	**12** canyon		catarata (grande)	
duna	**13** dune/sand dune			

A.
{ This is a beautiful _____!
{ These are beautiful _____s!

B. I agree. It's/They're magnificent!

Tell about the geography of your country. Describe the different geographic features.

Have you seen some of the geographic features in this lesson? Which ones? Where?

CIENCIAS

Equipo para el laboratorio de ciencias / Science Equipment

microscopio	**1**	microscope
computadora/ordenador	**2**	computer
platina	**3**	slide
caja de Petri/de cultivos	**4**	Petri dish
matraz	**5**	flask
embudo	**6**	funnel
vaso de precipitados	**7**	beaker
tubo de ensayo/probeta	**8**	test tube
fórceps/tenazas	**9**	forceps
pinzas para crisol	**10**	crucible tongs
mechero de Bunsen	**11**	Bunsen burner
probeta graduada	**12**	graduated cylinder
imán	**13**	magnet
prisma	**14**	prism
gotero	**15**	dropper
productos químicos	**16**	chemicals
balanza/báscula	**17**	balance
balanza/báscula	**18**	scale

El método científico / The Scientific Method

presentar el problema	**A**	state the problem
formular una hipótesis	**B**	form a hypothesis
planear un procedimiento	**C**	plan a procedure
realizar el procedimiento	**D**	do a procedure
anotar las observaciones	**E**	make/record observations
sacar conclusiones	**F**	draw conclusions

A. What do we need to do this procedure?
B. We need a/an/the ___[1–18]___ .

A. How is your experiment coming along?
B. I'm getting ready to ___[A–F]___ .

Do you have experience with the scientific equipment in this lesson? Tell about it.

What science courses do/did you take in school?

Think of an idea for a science experiment.
What question about science do you want to answer? State the problem.
What do you think will happen in the experiment? Form a hypothesis.
How can you test your hypothesis? Plan a procedure.

OCCUPATIONS I

PROFESIONES Y OFICIOS I

contador/contable	**1** accountant		hombre de negocios	**10** businessman
actor	**2** actor		mujer de negocios	**11** businesswoman
actriz	**3** actress		carnicero(a)	**12** butcher
pintor(a)	**4** artist		carpintero(a)	**13** carpenter
montador(a)/ ensamblador(a)/ armador(a)	**5** assembler		cajero(a)	**14** cashier
			chef/cocinero(a)	**15** chef/cook
niñero(a)/canguro	**6** babysitter		auxiliar de guardería infantil	**16** child day-care worker
panadero(a)	**7** baker		ingeniero(a) de informática	**17** computer software engineer
peluquero(a)/barbero(a)	**8** barber			
albañil	**9** bricklayer/ mason		obrero(a)	**18** construction worker

[1–5]
A. What do you do?
B. I'm an **accountant**.

[6–18]
A. What do you do?
B. I'm a **babysitter**.

Which of these occupations do you think is the most interesting? Why?

OCCUPATIONS II

PROFESIONES Y OFICIOS II

portero(a)/ afanador(a) **1** custodian/ janitor

anotador(a) de datos **2** data entry clerk

repartidor(a) **3** delivery person

estibador(a) **4** dockworker

obrero(a) **5** factory worker

granjero(a)/agricultor(a) **6** farmer

bombero(a) **7** firefighter

pescador(a) **8** fisher

empleado(a) de cafetería **9** food-service worker

maestro(a) de obras/ capataz **10** foreman

jardinero(a)/ paisajista **11** gardener/ landscaper

costurero(a) **12** garment worker

peluquero(a) **13** hairdresser

ayudante/ asistente de salud **14** health-care aide/ attendant

ayudante/asistente de salud en casa **15** home health aide/ home attendant

encargado(a) de la casa/ amo(a) de casa **16** homemaker

A. What do you do?
B. I'm a **custodian**.

Which of these occupations do you think is the most difficult? Why?

OCCUPATIONS III

PROFESIONES Y OFICIOS III

sirviente(a)/criado(a)/ **1** housekeeper
empleado(a) de servicio
doméstico

abogado(a) **2** lawyer

maquinista **3** machine operator

cartero(a) **4** mail carrier/
letter carrier

director(a)/gerente/ **5** manager
administrador(a)

manicurista **6** manicurist

mecánico(a) **7** mechanic

técnico(a) sanitario(a)/ **8** medical assistant/
asistente médico(a) physician assistant

mensajero(a) **9** messenger/
courier

mozo(a) de mudanzas **10** mover

pintor(a) **11** painter

boticario(a)/ **12** pharmacist
farmacéutico(a)/
farmacista

fotógrafo(a) **13** photographer

piloto **14** pilot

policía **15** police officer

recepcionista/ **16** receptionist
recepcionista-
telefonista

A. What's your occupation?
B. I'm a **housekeeper**.
A. A **housekeeper**?
B. Yes. That's right.

Which of these occupations do you think is the most important? Why?

PROFESIONES Y OFICIOS IV

reparador(a)/mecánico(a) **1** repairperson

vendedor(a) **2** salesperson

basurero(a)/ **3** sanitation worker/
recolector(a) de basura   trash collector

secretario(a) **4** secretary

guardia de seguridad **5** security guard

soldado **6** serviceman

soldada **7** servicewoman

empleado(a) de almacén **8** stock clerk

tendero(a)/ **9** store owner/
comerciante   shopkeeper

supervisor(a) **10** supervisor

sastre(a) **11** tailor

maestro(a)/ **12** teacher/
profesor(a)   instructor

traductor(a)/ **13** translator/
intérprete   interpreter

camionero(a) **14** truck driver

veterinario(a) **15** veterinarian/vet

mesero/camarero **16** waiter/server

mesera/camarera **17** waitress/server

soldador(a) **18** welder

A. What do you do?
B. I'm a **repairperson**. How about you?
A. I'm a **secretary**.

Do you work? What's your occupation? What are the occupations of the people in your family?

JOB SKILLS AND ACTIVITIES I

ACTIVIDADES RELACIONADAS CON EL TRABAJO I

actuar	**1** act	archivar	**10** file
armar/montar *componentes*	**2** assemble *components*	pilotear *un avión*	**11** fly *an airplane*
ayudar a *pacientes*	**3** assist *patients*	cultivar *vegetales*	**12** grow *vegetables*
hacer/construir *cosas*	**4** build *things*/ construct *things*	vigilar/cuidar *edificios*	**13** guard *buildings*
limpiar	**5** clean	administrar *un restaurante*	**14** manage *a restaurant*
cocinar	**6** cook	cortar *el césped*	**15** mow *lawns*
repartir *pizzas*	**7** deliver *pizzas*	manejar *herramientas*/ *máquinas*	**16** operate *equipment*
dibujar/trazar	**8** draw		
manejar/conducir *un camión*	**9** drive *a truck*		

A. Can you **act**?
B. Yes, I can.

Can you do any of these activities? Which ones?

ACTIVIDADES RELACIONADAS CON EL TRABAJO II

Spanish	#	English
pintar	1	paint
preparar *comida*	2	prepare *food*
reparar/componer/arreglar *cosas*	3	repair *things*/fix *things*
vender *autos/carros/coches*	4	sell *cars*
servir *la comida*	5	serve *food*
coser	6	sew
hablar *español*	7	speak *Spanish*
supervisar *empleados*	8	supervise *people*
cuidar a *gente mayor*	9	take care of *elderly people*
hacer inventario	10	take inventory
enseñar	11	teach
traducir	12	translate
mecanografiar/teclear	13	type
usar *una caja registradora*	14	use *a cash register*
lavar *platos*	15	wash *dishes*
escribir	16	write

A. Do you know how to **paint**?
B. Yes, I do.

Tell about your job skills. What can you do?

EN BUSCA DE EMPLEO

Tipos de anuncios	Types of Job Ads	En busca de empleo	Job Search
letrero de se busca ayuda	**1** help wanted sign	responder a un anuncio	**A** respond to an ad
tablero de anuncios	**2** job notice / job announcement	solicitar información	**B** request information
		solicitar una entrevista	**C** request an interview
anuncio/clasificado/ de empleo	**3** classified ad / want ad	preparar el currículum vítae	**D** prepare a resume
		vestirse de manera apropiada	**E** dress appropriately
Abreviaturas en los anuncios	**Job Ad Abbreviations**	llenar una solicitud	**F** fill out an application (form)
tiempo completo	**4** full-time	ir a una entrevista	**G** go to an interview
tiempo parcial/ medio tiempo	**5** part-time	hablar sobre sus aptitudes y habilidades	**H** talk about your skills and qualifications
disponible	**6** available	hablar sobre su experiencia laboral	**I** talk about your experience
por hora	**7** hour	pedir información acerca del sueldo	**J** ask about the salary
de lunes a viernes	**8** Monday through Friday		
por las tardes	**9** evenings	pedir información acerca de los subsidios y prestaciones laborales	**K** ask about the benefits
previo(a)	**10** previous		
experiencia	**11** experience	escribir una nota de agradecimiento	**L** write a thank-you note
se requiere	**12** required	ser contratado(a)/nombrado(a)	**M** get hired
excelente	**13** excellent		

A. How did you find your job?
B. I found it through a ___[1–3]___.

A. How was your job interview?
B. It went very well.
A. Did you ___[D–F, H–M]___?
B. Yes, I did.

Tell about a job you are familiar with. What are the skills and qualifications required for the job? What are the hours? What is the salary?

Tell about how people you know found their jobs.

Tell about your own experience with a job search or a job interview.

THE FACTORY

LA FÁBRICA

reloj marcador/checador	**1** time clock	embalador(a)/empacador(a)	**12** packer
tarjetas de asistencia	**2** time cards	portacarga/montacarga	**13** forklift
vestidor	**3** locker room	ascensor de carga	**14** freight elevator
cadena/línea de montaje	**4** (assembly) line	circular del sindicato	**15** union notice
obrero(a)/operario(a)	**5** (factory) worker	buzón de sugerencias	**16** suggestion box
estación de trabajo	**6** work station	sección/departamento de envíos	**17** shipping department
supervisor(a) de cadena de montaje	**7** line supervisor	encargado(a) de envíos	**18** shipping clerk
supervisor(a) de control de calidad	**8** quality control supervisor	carrito manual/diablito	**19** hand truck/dolly
máquina	**9** machine	muelle de carga	**20** loading dock
cinta transportadora	**10** conveyor belt	oficina de pagos/de nómina	**21** payroll office
almacén/depósito	**11** warehouse	oficina de personal	**22** personnel office

A. Excuse me. I'm a new employee.
Where's/Where are the _____?
B. Next to/Near/In/On the _____.

A. Where's *Tony*?
B. *He's* in/on/at/next to/near the _____.

Are there any factories where you live? What kind? What are the working conditions there?

What products do factories in your country produce?

THE CONSTRUCTION SITE

UN SITIO DE CONSTRUCCIÓN

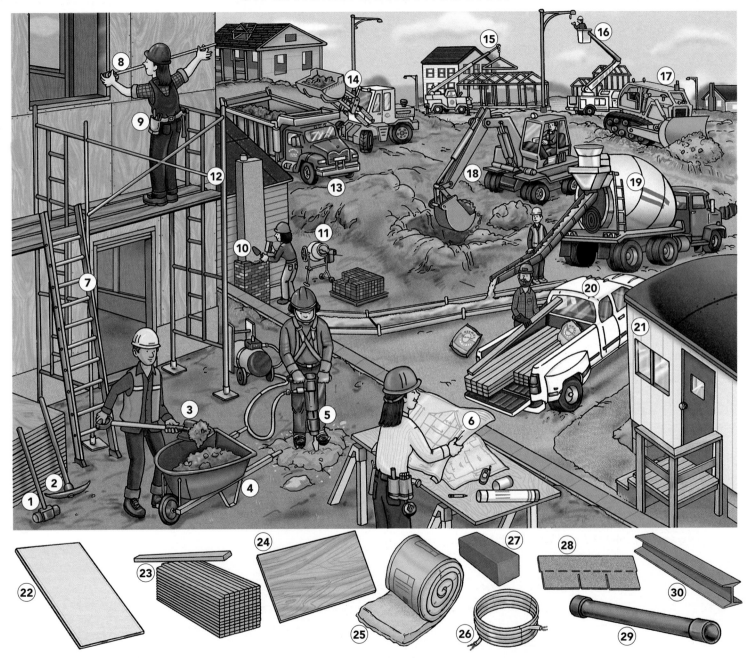

almádena/mazo	**1** sledgehammer	grúa (con plataforma movible)	**16** cherry picker	
pico	**2** pickax	bulldozer/tractor	**17** bulldozer	
pala	**3** shovel	tractor excavador(a)	**18** backhoe	
carretilla	**4** wheelbarrow	revolvedora de concreto/	**19** concrete mixer	
taladro/neumático	**5** jackhammer/	hormigonera	truck	
perforador	pneumatic drill	camioneta de carga/pickup	**20** pickup truck	
planos	**6** blueprints	casa remolque/tráiler	**21** trailer	
escalera	**7** ladder	muro en seco/	**22** drywall	
cinta métrica	**8** tape measure	muro ensamblable		
cinturón para herramientas	**9** toolbelt	madera	**23** wood/lumber	
palustre/paleta/llana	**10** trowel	madera contrachapada	**24** plywood	
mezcladora de	**11** cement mixer	fibra aislante	**25** insulation	
cemento/mortero		alambre	**26** wire	
andamio	**12** scaffolding	ladrillo	**27** brick	
volquete	**13** dump truck	teja	**28** shingle	
pala cargadora mecánica	**14** front-end loader	tubo	**29** pipe	
grúa	**15** crane	viga/trabe	**30** girder/beam	

A. Could you get me
   that/those ___[1–10]___?
B. Sure.

A. Watch out for that ___[11–21]___!
B. Oh! Thanks for the warning!

A. Do we have enough
   ___[22–26]___ / ___[27–30]___s?
B. I think so.

What building materials is your home made of?

Describe a construction site near your home or school.
Tell about the construction equipment and the materials.

JOB SAFETY

SEGURIDAD LABORAL

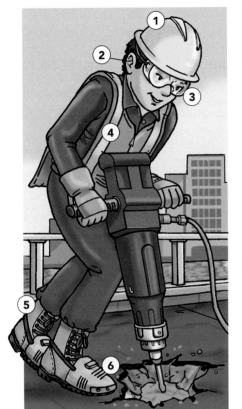

1
2
3
4
5
6

7

8

9
10
11

12

13

14

15

16

17

18 **DANGER**

19 **CAUTION HAZARDOUS AREA**

20

21

22

23

EXIT

25 **ALARM WILL SOUND**

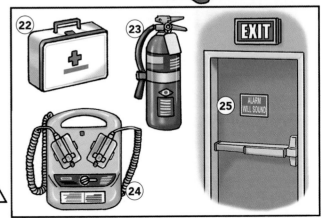

24

Spanish	No.	English
casco de construcción	1	hard hat / helmet
tapones para oídos	2	earplugs
anteojos/gafas de seguridad	3	goggles
chaleco de seguridad	4	safety vest
botas protectoras	5	safety boots
protector para los dedos de los pies	6	toe guard
faja/arnés de soporte	7	back support
orejeras protectoras	8	safety earmuffs
redecilla	9	hairnet
mascarilla/máscara	10	mask
guantes de látex	11	latex gloves
mascarilla filtrante	12	respirator
visor para soldar/ gafas de seguridad	13	safety glasses

Spanish	No.	English
inflamable	14	flammable
venenoso(a)	15	poisonous
corrosivo(a)	16	corrosive
radioactivo(a)	17	radioactive
peligroso(a)	18	dangerous
peligroso(a)	19	hazardous
agente biológico infeccioso/ patógeno tóxico	20	biohazard
peligro de electrocución	21	electrical hazard
botiquín/maletín de primeros auxilios	22	first-aid kit
extinguidor/ extintor de incendios	23	fire extinguisher
desfibrilador	24	defibrillator
salida de emergencia	25	emergency exit

A. Don't forget to wear your __[1–13]__!
B. Thanks for reminding me.

A. Be careful!
That material is __[14–17]__!
That machine is __[18]__!
That work area is __[19]__!
That's a __[20]__! / That's an __[21]__!
B. Thanks for the warning.

A. Where's the __[22–25]__?
B. It's over there.

Do you / Did you ever use any of the safety equipment in this lesson? When? Where?

Where do you see safety equipment in your community?

PUBLIC TRANSPORTATION

EL TRANSPORTE PÚBLICO

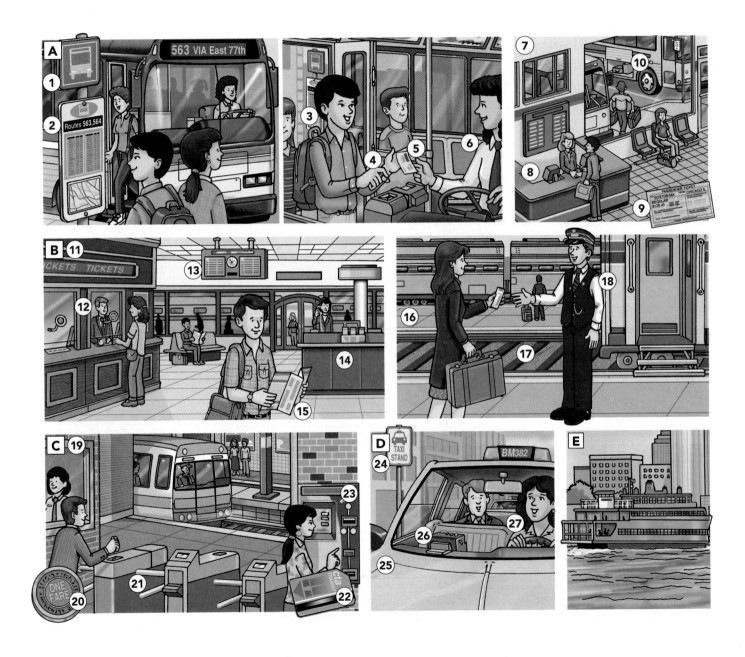

autobús/bus/guagua/camión	**A**	**bus**
parada/paradero	**1**	bus stop
ruta	**2**	bus route
pasàjero(a)	**3**	passenger
tarifa	**4**	(bus) fare
billete de trasbordo	**5**	transfer
conductor(a)/chofer de autobús/busero(a)	**6**	bus driver
estación de autobuses	**7**	bus station
boletería/taquilla	**8**	ticket counter
billete/pasaje/boleto	**9**	ticket
maletero	**10**	baggage compartment

tren	**B**	**train**
estación de trenes	**11**	train station
taquilla/ventanilla	**12**	ticket window
tablero de llegadas y salidas	**13**	arrival and departure board
mostrador de información	**14**	information booth
horarios	**15**	schedule/timetable

andén	**16**	platform
riel/vía	**17**	track
cobrador(a)	**18**	conductor

metro/subterráneo	**C**	**subway**
estación del metro	**19**	subway station
ficha	**20**	(subway) token
torniquete/contador de entrada	**21**	turnstile
tarjeta de pasaje/ boleto prepagado	**22**	fare card
máquina expendedora de pasajes/boletos	**23**	fare card machine

taxi	**D**	**taxi**
parada de taxis/piquera	**24**	taxi stand
taxi	**25**	taxi/cab
taxímetro	**26**	meter
taxista/chofer de taxi	**27**	cab driver/taxi driver

transbordador/ferry	**E**	**ferry**

[A–E]

A. How are you going to get there?

B. { I'm going to take the ____[A–C, E]____ .
    I'm going to take a ____[D]____ .

[1, 7, 8, 10–19, 21, 23–25]

A. Excuse me. Where's the _____?

B. Over there.

How do you get to different places in your community? Describe public transportation where you live.

In your country, can you travel far by train or by bus? Where can you go? How much do tickets cost? Describe the buses and trains.

PREPOSITIONS OF MOTION

PREPOSICIONES PARA DAR DIRECCIONES

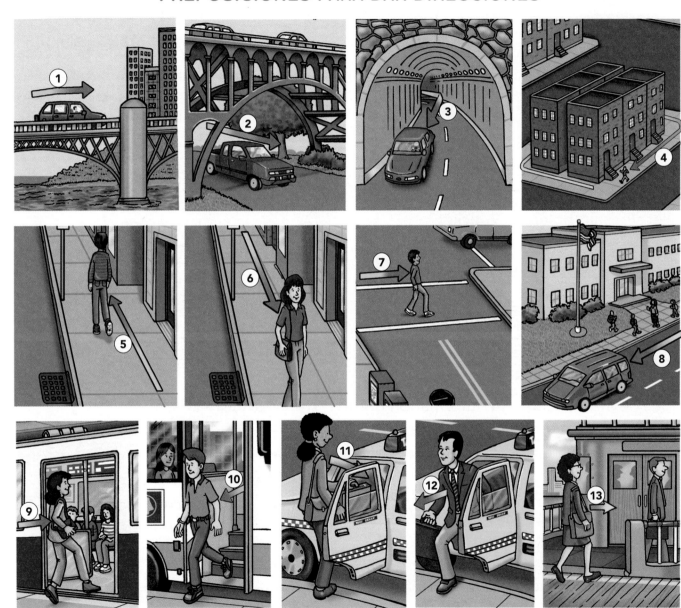

Spanish	#	English
cruzar el puente	**1**	over the bridge
bajo el puente	**2**	under the bridge
por el túnel	**3**	through the tunnel
doblar la esquina	**4**	around the corner
subir la calle	**5**	up the street
bajar la calle	**6**	down the street
cruzar la calle	**7**	across the street
más allá de *la escuela*	**8**	past the *school*

Spanish	#	English
subir a	**9**	on
bajar de	**10**	off
entrar en	**11**	into
salir de	**12**	out of
entrar en	**13**	onto

[1–8]
A. Go **over** the bridge.
B. **Over** the bridge?
A. Yes.

[9–13]
A. I can't talk right now. I'm getting **on** a train.
B. You're getting **on** a train?
A. Yes. I'll call you later.

What places do you go past on your way to school?

Tell how to get to different places from your home or your school.

TRAFFIC SIGNS AND DIRECTIONS

SEÑALES E INDICACIONES/INSTRUCCIONES DE TRÁNSITO

Señales de tránsito	Traffic Signs
alto/stop	**1** stop
no doble a la izquierda	**2** no left turn
no doble a la derecha	**3** no right turn
no doble en U	**4** no U-turn
doble sólo a la derecha	**5** right turn only
prohibido el paso	**6** do not enter
un solo sentido	**7** one way
calle sin salida	**8** dead end/no outlet
cruce de peatones	**9** pedestrian crossing
cruce de rieles/de ferrocarril	**10** railroad crossing
cruce escolar	**11** school crossing
unión de carriles	**12** merging traffic
ceda el paso	**13** yield
desvío	**14** detour
resbaladizo(a) si está mojado(a)	**15** slippery when wet
estacionamiento para discapacitados(as)	**16** handicapped parking only

Direcciones de la brújula	Compass Directions
norte	**17** north
sur	**18** south
oeste/poniente	**19** west
este/oriente	**20** east

Instrucciones para el examen de manejar/conducir	Road Test Instructions
Doble a la izquierda.	**21** Turn left.
Doble a la derecha.	**22** Turn right.
Siga derecho/recto.	**23** Go straight.
Estaciónese paralelo a la acera.	**24** Parallel park.
Dé un viraje de tres puntos.	**25** Make a 3-point turn.
Use señales de mano.	**26** Use hand signals.

[1–16]
A. Careful! That sign says "**stop**"!
B. Oh. Thanks.

[17–20]
A. Which way should I go?
B. Go **north**.

[21–26]
A. Turn **right**.
B. Turn **right**?
A. Yes.

Which of these traffic signs are in your neighborhood? What other traffic signs do you usually see?

Describe any differences between traffic signs in different countries you know.

THE AIRPORT
EL AEROPUERTO

A
ARRIVALS   DEPARTURES
3 1
2
4
5

B
6 7
8
9
10

C
NORTHEAST AIR
NE
40 BOSTON 7:45   41 LONDON 7:55
41
13
14
11
12

NORTHEAST AIRLINES
NORTHEAST AIRLINES
BOARDING PASS   GROUP 1
seat 27D
FLIGHT 1062
ROW SEAT
27   D

D
15
16
17
18
19 LAX
FROM: TPA
TO: LAX
FLIGHT: 453

E
20 21
22
23
24
PASSPORT
25
26

Registro de pasajeros	A Check-In	Reclamo/Retiro de equipaje	D Baggage Claim
pasaje/boleto/billete	1 ticket	área de reclamo/ retiro de equipaje	15 baggage claim (area)
mostrador de pasajes	2 ticket counter	equipaje	16 baggage
expendedor(a) de pasajes	3 ticket agent	carretilla/carrito para equipaje	17 luggage carrier
maleta/valija/petaca	4 suitcase		
monitor de llegadas y salidas	5 arrival and departure monitor	bolsa para trajes/ vestidos/sacos y abrigos	18 garment bag
		etiqueta/boleto de factura de equipaje	19 baggage claim check

Seguridad — **B Security**

- control de seguridad — **6** security checkpoint
- detector de metales — **7** metal detector
- guardia de seguridad — **8** security officer
- máquina de rayos X — **9** X-ray machine
- equipaje de mano — **10** carry-on bag

Inmigración y aduana	E Customs and Immigration
aduana	20 customs
empleado(a) de aduana	21 customs officer
tarjeta/formulario de declaración de aduana	22 customs declaration form
inmigración	23 immigration
oficial de inmigración	24 immigration officer
pasaporte	25 passport
visa	26 visa

La puerta/sala (de embarque y desembarque) — **C The Gate**

- mostrador de factura/registro/ chequeo — **11** check-in counter
- tarjeta de abordaje — **12** boarding pass
- puerta/sala — **13** gate
- área de abordaje — **14** boarding area

[2, 3, 5–9, 11, 13–15, 20, 21, 23, 24]
A. Excuse me. Where's the _____?*
B. Right over there.

* *With 20 and 23, use:* Excuse me. Where's _____?

[1, 4, 10, 12, 16–19, 22, 25, 26]
A. Oh, no! I can't find my _____!
B. I'll help you look for it.

Describe an airport you are familiar with. Tell about the check-in area, the security area, the gates, and the baggage claim area.

Tell about a time you went through Customs and Immigration.

PLACES TO GO

LUGARES DE DIVERSIÓN

museo	**1** museum		parque	**11** park
galería de arte	**2** art gallery		playa	**12** beach
concierto	**3** concert		montañas	**13** mountains
obra de teatro	**4** play		acuario	**14** aquarium
parque de diversiones	**5** amusement park		jardín botánico	**15** botanical gardens
sitio histórico	**6** historic site		planetario	**16** planetarium
parque nacional	**7** national park		zoológico	**17** zoo
feria de artesanías	**8** craft fair		cine	**18** movies
venta de patio	**9** yard sale		feria ambulante	**19** carnival
mercado de pulgas/ mercadillo/tianguis	**10** swap meet / flea market		exposición/feria	**20** fair

A. What do you want to do today?

B. Let's go to $\begin{cases} \text{a/an } \underline{\quad[1-9]\quad}. \\ \text{the } \underline{\quad[10-20]\quad}. \end{cases}$

A. What did you do over the weekend?

B. I went to $\begin{cases} \text{a/an } \underline{\quad[1-9]\quad}. \\ \text{the } \underline{\quad[10-20]\quad}. \end{cases}$

A. What are you going to do on your day off?

B. I'm going to go to $\begin{cases} \text{a/an } \underline{\quad[1-9]\quad}. \\ \text{the } \underline{\quad[10-20]\quad}. \end{cases}$

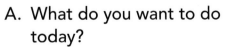

What are some of your favorite places to go? Where are they? What do you do there?

DEPORTES Y ACTIVIDADES INDIVIDUALES

footing/correr al trote/trotar	**1** jogging	pelota vasca/frontón de raqueta	**11** racquetball
correr	**2** running	tenis de mesa/pimpón/ ping-pong	**12** table tennis / ping pong
caminar	**3** walking		
patinaje/patinar	**4** inline skating / rollerblading	golf	**13** golf
		billar	**14** billiards/pool
ciclismo	**5** cycling/biking	artes marciales	**15** martial arts
andar en patineta/monopatín	**6** skateboarding	gimnasia	**16** gymnastics
jugar a los bolos/al boliche	**7** bowling	levantar pesas	**17** weightlifting
montar a caballo	**8** horseback riding	hacer ejercicio(s)	**18** work out/exercise
tenis	**9** tennis	boxear	**19** box
bádminton	**10** badminton	practicar lucha libre	**20** wrestle

[1–8]

A. What do you like to do in your free time?
B. I like to go **jogging**.

[9–14]

A. What do you like to do on the weekend?
B. I like to play **tennis**.

[15–17]

A. What do you like to do for exercise?
B. I like to do **martial arts**.

[18–20]

A. Do you exercise regularly?
B. Yes. I **work out** three times a week.

Do you do any of these activities? Which ones?

Which of these activities are popular in your country?

TEAM SPORTS

DEPORTES EN EQUIPO

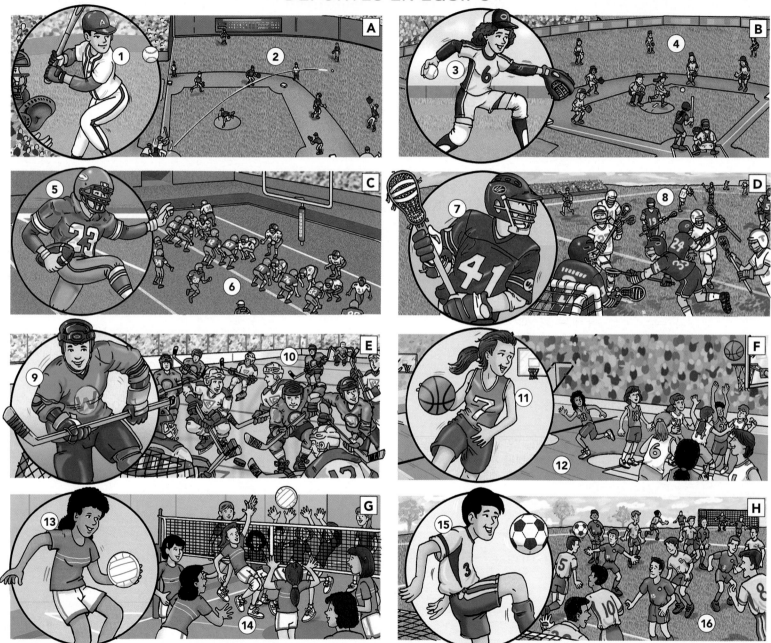

béisbol	**A baseball**	**hockey sobre hielo**	**E (ice) hockey**
jugador(a) de béisbol	1 baseball player	jugador(a) de hockey	9 hockey player
campo de juego/ diamante de béisbol	2 baseball field / ballfield	pista de hielo	10 hockey rink
softball/sófbol	**B softball**	**baloncesto/básquetbol**	**F basketball**
jugador(a) de sófbol	3 softball player	jugador(a) de baloncesto/básquetbol	11 basketball player
campo de sófbol	4 ballfield	cancha/pista de baloncesto/básquetbol	12 basketball court
fútbol americano	**C football**	**voleibol/balonvolea**	**G volleyball**
jugador(a) de fútbol americano	5 football player	jugador(a) de voleibol	13 volleyball player
campo de fútbol americano	6 football field	cancha de voleibol	14 volleyball court
lacrosse/cross	**D lacrosse**	**fútbol/balompié/sóquer**	**H soccer**
jugador(a) de lacrosse	7 lacrosse player	jugador(a) de fútbol	15 soccer player
campo de lacrosse	8 lacrosse field	campo de fútbol	16 soccer field

[A–H]

A. Do you like to play **baseball**?
B. Yes. **Baseball** is one of my favorite sports.

A. .... plays __[A–H]__ very well.
B. You're right. I think he's/she's the best _____* on the team.

*Use 1, 3, 5, 7, 9, 11, 13, 15.

A. Now listen, team! Go out on that _____† and play the best game of __[A–H]__ you can!
B. All right, Coach!

† Use 2, 4, 6, 8, 10, 12, 14, 16.

Which sports in this lesson do you like to play? Which do you like to watch?

What are your favorite teams?

Name some famous players of these sports.

ENTERTAINMENT

DIVERSIONES

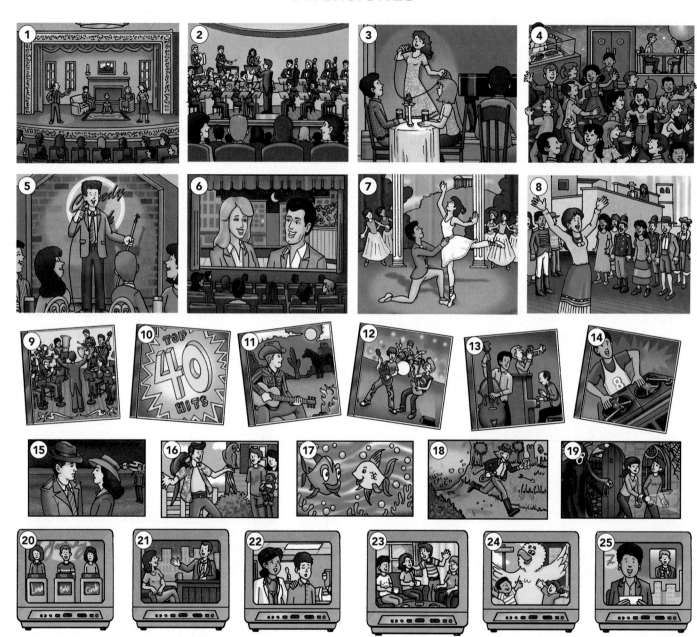

obra de teatro	**1** play	música country	**11** country music	películas de horror	**19** horror movie
concierto	**2** concert	música rock	**12** rock music		
club nocturno/cabaré con música viva	**3** music club	jazz	**13** jazz	**programas de televisión**	**TV programs**
		hip hop	**14** hip hop		
club de baile/ discoteca	**4** dance club	**películas**	**movies/films**	programas concurso/de juegos	**20** game show/ quiz show
club nocturno/cabaré con programa de cómicos	**5** comedy club	dramas	**15** drama	programas de entrevistas/opinión	**21** talk show
		comedias	**16** comedy		
películas	**6** movies	dibujos/ viñetas/ caricaturas animadas(os)	**17** cartoon	dramas	**22** drama
ballet	**7** ballet			comedias	**23** (situation) comedy/ sitcom
ópera	**8** opera	películas de aventuras/ de acción	**18** action movie/ adventure movie		
música	**music**			programas infantiles	**24** children's program
música clásica	**9** classical music				
música popular	**10** popular music			noticieros/ telediarios	**25** news program

[1–8]
A. What are you doing this evening?
B. I'm going to { a _____[1–5]_____ .
the _____[6–8]_____ .

[9–14]
A. What kind of music do you like?
B. I like **classical music**.

[15–19]
A. What kind of movies do you like?
B. I like **drama**s.

[20–25]
A. What kind of TV programs do you like to watch?
B. I like to watch **talk show**s.

What kinds of entertainment in this lesson do you like?
What kinds of entertainment are popular in your country?

What's your favorite type of music? Who is your favorite singer? musician? musical group?

What kind of movies do you like?
Who are you favorite movie stars?
What are the titles of your favorite movies?

What kind of TV programs do you like? What are your favorite shows?

FORMAS PARA IDENTIFICARSE

1
Florida The Sunshine State
DRIVER LICENSE CLASS D
D200-555-44-111-0
Dawn Erics
220 Palisades Way
Miami, FL 33017-0000
DOB: 05-20-65   SEX: F   HGT: 5-07
ISSUED: 05-19-05
EXPIRES: 05-20-11
REST: BF
DORSE.
Dawn Erics
ORGAN DONOR
Q123456789000   SAFE DRIVER
Operation of a motor vehicle constitutes consent to any sobriety test required by law.

2
SOCIAL SECURITY
142-84-5194
THIS NUMBER HAS BEEN ESTABLISHED FOR
PATRICK MICHAEL GAFFNEY
Patrick Michael Gaffney
SIGNATURE

3
International *Student* Identity Card
Carte d'étudiant internationale / Carné internacional de estudiante
STUDENT
Studies at / Étudiant à / Est. de Enseñanza
School of Audio Engineering
Name / Nom / Nombre
Robert Oliver
Born /Né(e) le / Nacido/a el
19 FEB 1986
Validity / Validité / Validez
09/2005 - 12/2006
ISIC
S 044 201 440 365

4
Global Computer
Dawn Erics
Associate Sales Manager
ID# 752-775-754-752

5
PERMANENT RESIDENT CARD
NAME   RIVERA, CARLOS M.
INS A#   A92475816
Birthdate   Category   Sex
03/17/66   IR6   M
Country of Birth
Mexico
CARD EXPIRES   06/29/09
Resident Since   11/17/99
C1USA0924758166EAC0013440673<<
6003029M1004268MEX<<<<<<<<<<<0
RIVERA<<CARLOS<<<<<<<<<<<<<<

6
PASSPORT
United States
of America

7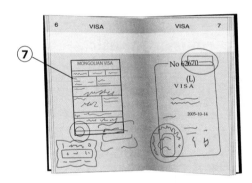
VISA   VISA
MONGOLIAN VISA
No 62670
(L)
VISA
2005-10-14

8
WORK PERMIT
INDIVIDUAL WORK PERMIT:
1. Employer completes and signs
2. Parent or guardian completes and signs
3. Employer submits work permit and LEGIBLE copy of minor's proof of age to the Wage and Hour office.
4. When the approved work permit is returned, the minor may begin work.

GENERAL DUTIES WORK PERMIT:
1. Employer completes and signs
2. Employer submits work permit to Wage and Hour office.
3. The approved duties are returned to the employer. After employer obtains the signature of the minor's parent or guardian then the minor may begin work.
4. Employer must return a copy of the work permit signed by the parent or legal guardian and LEGIBLE copy of proof of age to the Wage and Hour office within seven (7) calendar days of minor beginning work.

☐ INDIVIDUAL WORK PERMIT
☐ GENERAL DUTIES WORK PERMIT APPROVED FOR:
☐ 16 & 17 YEAR OLDS; OR
☐ 14 - 17 YEAR OLDS
☐ APPROVED AS AMENDED
☐ DISAPPROVED
By: _____
Date: _____

Return permit to employer's FAX number:
_____

Section (A) to be completed by EMPLOYER
Name of Employer | DBA/
Employer's Local Mailing Address: | City: | Zip

9
◆ Voltage Electric Bill
Voltage Electric
20 Spring Street
Paramus, NJ

Service At:
Robert Smith
33 Catherine Rd
Paramus, NJ

Customer Account Number
123456789
Due Date: Amount Due:
January 15, 2005 $35.00

Previous Charges
	Account Balance	Amount Due
Total Amount of Last Bill	$ 35.00	
Payment 12/15/04	$ 35.00	
Previous Balance	$ .00	$ .00

Current Charges
Customer Charge	$ 4.75
Delivery Charge	$ 12.80

10
CERTIFICATE OF BIRTH
(In the Clerks office of the County Commision of Randolf County)

I, MARK PALMER, Clerk of the County Commision in the County and State aforesaid, it being an office of record, and having a seal, do hereby certify that the records in my office show that _____ Sex _____
Was born at _____ in Bergen County and the State of New Jersey on the _____ day of _____ and that the parents names are as follows:
Father's name _____
Mother's maiden name _____
are recorded in Birth Record No. _____ at page _____ Date filed: _____

In testimony whereof, I have hereunto affixed my signature and official seal at Bergen County, NJ this _____ day of _____ 20 _____
_____, Clerk

licencia para manejar/conducir	**1** driver's license
tarjeta de seguro social	**2** social security card
carné/credencial de estudiante	**3** student I.D. card
tarjeta de identificación de empleado(a)	**4** employee I.D. badge
tarjeta de residente permanente	**5** permanent resident card
pasaporte	**6** passport
visa	**7** visa
permiso de trabajo	**8** work permit
comprobante de residencia	**9** proof of residence
certificado de nacimiento	**10** birth certificate

A. May I see your _____?
B. Yes. Here you are.

A. Oh, no! I can't find my _____!
B. I'll help you look for it.
A. Thanks.

Which forms of identification do you have? When do you need to show them?

U.S. GOVERNMENT

LA ORGANIZACIÓN DEL GOBIERNO DE LOS ESTADOS UNIDOS

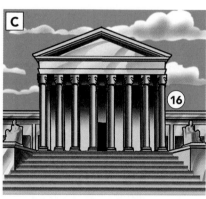

El poder legislativo	**A**	**legislative branch**
hace las leyes	**1**	makes the laws
representantes/congresistas	**2**	representatives/congressmen and congresswomen
Cámara de Representantes	**3**	house of representatives
senadores(as)	**4**	senators
Senado	**5**	senate
Edificio del Capitolio	**6**	Capitol Building

El poder ejecutivo	**B**	**executive branch**
hace cumplir las leyes	**7**	enforces the laws
presidente(a)	**8**	president

vicepresidente(a)	**9**	vice-president
gabinete (cuerpo de ministros(as))	**10**	cabinet
Casa Blanca	**11**	White House

El poder judicial	**C**	**judicial branch**
explica las leyes	**12**	explains the laws
jueces/juezas de la Corte Suprema de Justicia	**13**	Supreme Court justices
Presidente(a) de la Corte Suprema de Justicia	**14**	chief justice
Corte Suprema de Justicia	**15**	Supreme Court
Edificio de la Corte Suprema de Justicia	**16**	Supreme Court Building

A. Which branch of government __[1, 7, 12]__?
B. The __[A, B, C]__.

A. Who works in the __[A, B, C]__ of the government?
B. The __[2, 4, 8–10, 13, 14]__.

A. Where do/does the __[2, 4, 8–10, 13, 14]__ work?
B. In the __[6, 11, 16]__.

A. In which branch of the government is the __[3, 5, 10, 15]__?
B. In the __[A, B, C]__.

Compare the governments of different countries you are familiar with. What are the branches of government? Who works there? What do they do?

La Constitución A The Constitution

la Carta Magna **1** "the supreme law of the land"

el Preámbulo **2** the Preamble

La Declaración de Derechos B The Bill of Rights

las primeras diez enmiendas a la Constitución **3** the first 10 amendments to the Constitution

La primera enmienda C The 1st Amendment

libertad de expresión **4** freedom of speech

libertad de prensa **5** freedom of the press

libertad de credo **6** freedom of religion

derecho a participar en asambleas **7** freedom of assembly

Otras enmiendas D Other Amendments

pusieron fin a la esclavitud **8** ended slavery

otorgaron el derecho a votar a los/las afroamericanos(as) **9** gave African-Americans the right to vote

establecieron impuestos sobre los ingresos **10** established income taxes

otorgaron el derecho a votar a las mujeres **11** gave women the right to vote

otorgaron el derecho a votar a los/las ciudadanos(as) mayores de dieciocho años **12** gave citizens eighteen years and older the right to vote

---

A. What is ___[A ,B]___ ?
B. ___[1 ,3]___ .

A. Which amendment guarantees people ___[4–7]___ ?
B. The 1st Amendment.

A. Which amendment ___[8–12]___ ?
B. The _____ Amendment.

A. What did the _____ Amendment do?
B. It ___[8–12]___ .

Describe how people in your community exercise their 1st Amendment rights. What are some examples of freedom of speech? the press? religion? assembly?

Do you have an idea for a new amendment? Tell about it and why you think it's important.

HOLIDAYS

DÍAS DE FIESTA

Año Nuevo	**1** New Year's Day
Día de Martin Luther King, Jr.	**2** Martin Luther King, Jr.* Day
Día de San Valentín	**3** Valentine's Day
Día del/de la Soldado(a)	**4** Memorial Day
Día de la Independencia/el Cuatro de Julio	**5** Independence Day/the Fourth of July
Halloween/Día de las Brujas	**6** Halloween
Día de los/las Veteranos(as)	**7** Veterans Day
Día de Acción de Gracias	**8** Thanksgiving
Navidad	**9** Christmas
Ramadán	**10** Ramadan
Kwanzaa	**11** Kwanzaa
Hanuka/Fiesta de las Luces	**12** Hanukkah

* Jr. = Junior

A. When is ___[1, 3, 5, 6, 7, 9]___ ?
B. It's on _(date)_ .

A. When is ___[2, 4, 8]___ ?
B. It's in _(month)_ .

A. When does ___[10–12]___
begin this year?
B. It begins on _(date)_ .

Which of these holidays do you celebrate? How?   What holidays do people celebrate in your country?

LOS ESTADOS UNIDOS Y EL CANADÁ

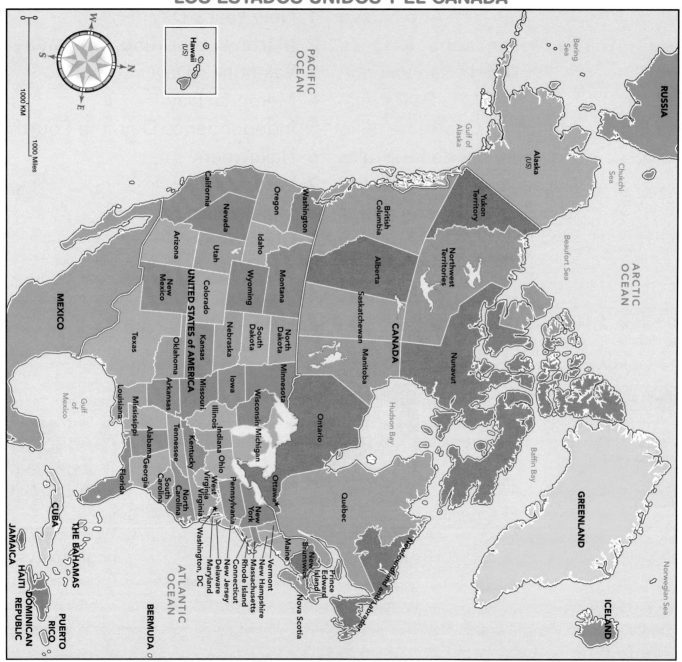

PACIFIC OCEAN

Hawaii (US)

Bering Sea

RUSSIA

Chukchi Sea

Gulf of Alaska

Alaska (US)

Yukon Territory

British Columbia

Beaufort Sea

ARCTIC OCEAN

Northwest Territories

California

Oregon

Washington

Nevada

Idaho

Alberta

MEXICO

Arizona

Utah

Montana

Wyoming

Saskatchewan

CANADA

Nunavut

New Mexico

Colorado

North Dakota

South Dakota

UNITED STATES of AMERICA

Kansas

Nebraska

Minnesota

Manitoba

Texas

Oklahoma

Missouri

Iowa

Wisconsin

Ontario

Hudson Bay

Baffin Bay

Arkansas

Illinois

Michigan

Louisiana

Mississippi

Alabama

Tennessee

Kentucky

Indiana

Ohio

Ottawa ★

Québec

GREENLAND

Gulf of Mexico

Florida

Georgia

South Carolina

North Carolina

West Virginia

Virginia

Pennsylvania

New York

Newfoundland and Labrador

CUBA

THE BAHAMAS

JAMAICA

HAITI

DOMINICAN REPUBLIC

PUERTO RICO

BERMUDA

ATLANTIC OCEAN

Washington, DC

Maryland

Delaware

New Jersey

Connecticut

Rhode Island

Massachusetts

New Hampshire

Vermont

Maine

New Brunswick

Prince Edward Island

Nova Scotia

Norwegian Sea

ICELAND

1000 KM

1000 Miles

MÉXICO, CENTROAMÉRICA Y EL CARIBE

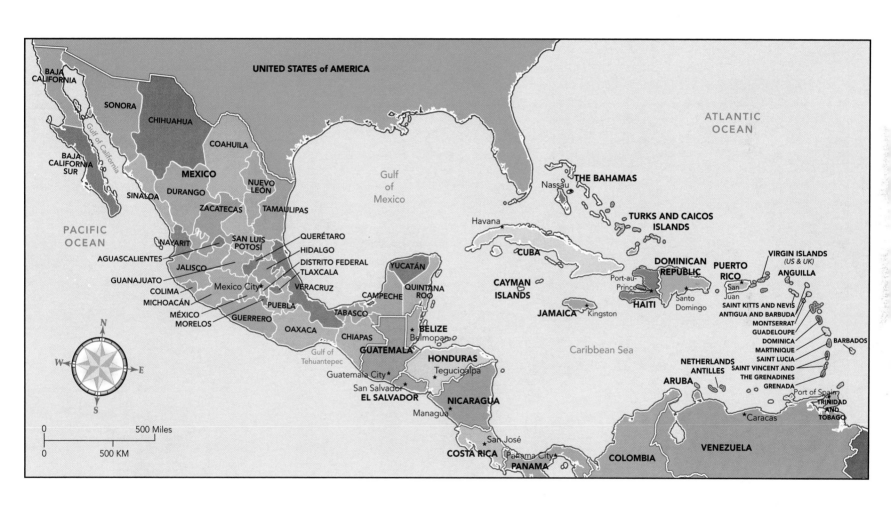

UNITED STATES of AMERICA

BAJA CALIFORNIA

SONORA

CHIHUAHUA

COAHUILA

BAJA CALIFORNIA SUR

Gulf of California

MEXICO

DURANGO

NUEVO LEÓN

SINALOA

ZACATECAS

TAMAULIPAS

PACIFIC OCEAN

NAYARIT

SAN LUIS POTOSÍ

QUERÉTARO

HIDALGO

AGUASCALIENTES

JALISCO

DISTRITO FEDERAL
TLAXCALA

GUANAJUATO

Mexico City

VERACRUZ

COLIMA

MICHOACÁN

MÉXICO
MORELOS

PUEBLA

GUERRERO

OAXACA

CHIAPAS

GUATEMALA

Gulf of Tehuantepec

Guatemala City

San Salvador
EL SALVADOR

CAMPECHE

TABASCO

YUCATÁN

QUINTANA ROO

BELIZE
Belmopan

HONDURAS

Tegucigalpa

NICARAGUA

Managua

San José

COSTA RICA

Panama City

PANAMA

Gulf of Mexico

Havana

CUBA

CAYMAN ISLANDS

JAMAICA

Kingston

Caribbean Sea

THE BAHAMAS

Nassau

TURKS AND CAICOS ISLANDS

DOMINICAN REPUBLIC

Port-au-Prince

HAITI

Santo Domingo

PUERTO RICO

San Juan

ATLANTIC OCEAN

VIRGIN ISLANDS
(US & UK)

ANGUILLA

SAINT KITTS AND NEVIS

ANTIGUA AND BARBUDA

MONTSERRAT

GUADELOUPE

DOMINICA

MARTINIQUE

SAINT LUCIA

SAINT VINCENT AND THE GRENADINES

GRENADA

BARBADOS

NETHERLANDS ANTILLES

ARUBA

Port of Spain

TRINIDAD AND TOBAGO

Caracas

COLOMBIA

VENEZUELA

N
W E
S

0   500 Miles
0   500 KM

THE WORLD

EL MUNDO

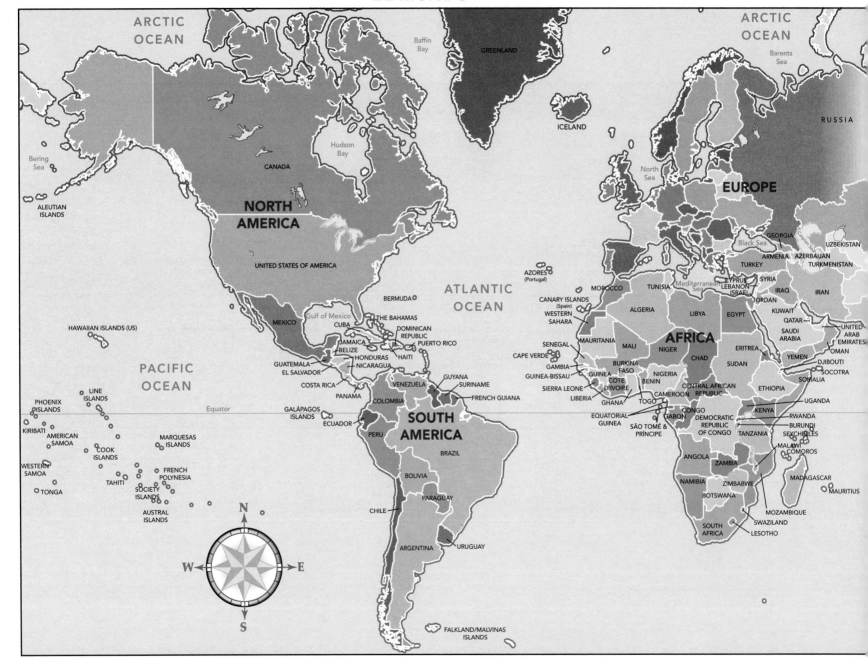

ARCTIC OCEAN

ARCTIC OCEAN

Baffin Bay

GREENLAND

ICELAND

Barents Sea

Bering Sea

ALEUTIAN ISLANDS

CANADA

Hudson Bay

North Sea

RUSSIA

NORTH AMERICA

EUROPE

UNITED STATES OF AMERICA

GEORGIA

Black Sea

UZBEKISTAN

ARMENIA AZERBAIJAN

TURKEY TURKMENISTAN

AZORES (Portugal)

ATLANTIC OCEAN

CYPRUS SYRIA

LEBANON IRAQ

ISRAEL IRAN

JORDAN

HAWAIIAN ISLANDS (US)

BERMUDA

Gulf of Mexico

MEXICO

THE BAHAMAS

CUBA

DOMINICAN REPUBLIC

JAMAICA PUERTO RICO

BELIZE HAITI

Mediterranean Sea

MOROCCO TUNISIA

CANARY ISLANDS (Spain)

WESTERN SAHARA

ALGERIA LIBYA EGYPT

KUWAIT

QATAR

SAUDI ARABIA

UNITED ARAB EMIRATES

OMAN

PACIFIC OCEAN

GUATEMALA

EL SALVADOR

HONDURAS

NICARAGUA

COSTA RICA

PANAMA

SENEGAL

CAPE VERDE

GAMBIA

GUINEA-BISSAU

MAURITANIA

MALI

AFRICA

NIGER

CHAD

ERITREA

SUDAN

YEMEN

DJIBOUTI

SOCOTRA

SOMALIA

ETHIOPIA

AFRICA

PHOENIX ISLANDS

LINE ISLANDS

Equator

GALÁPAGOS ISLANDS

ECUADOR

VENEZUELA

GUYANA

SURINAME

FRENCH GUIANA

COLOMBIA

SOUTH AMERICA

GUINEA

SIERRA LEONE

LIBERIA

COTE D'IVOIRE

GHANA

BURKINA FASO

BENIN

TOGO

NIGERIA

CAMEROON

CENTRAL AFRICAN REPUBLIC

EQUATORIAL GUINEA

SÃO TOMÉ & PRÍNCIPE

GABON

CONGO

DEMOCRATIC REPUBLIC OF CONGO

UGANDA

KENYA

RWANDA

BURUNDI

SEYCHELLES

TANZANIA

KIRIBATI

AMERICAN SAMOA

MARQUESAS ISLANDS

PERU

BRAZIL

COOK ISLANDS

WESTERN SAMOA

FRENCH POLYNESIA

BOLIVIA

ANGOLA

ZAMBIA

MALAWI

COMOROS

MADAGASCAR

MAURITIUS

TAHITI

SOCIETY ISLANDS

PARAGUAY

NAMIBIA

ZIMBABWE

TONGA

AUSTRAL ISLANDS

CHILE

BOTSWANA

MOZAMBIQUE

SWAZILAND

N

W E

S

ARGENTINA URUGUAY

SOUTH AFRICA

LESOTHO

FALKLAND/MALVINAS ISLANDS

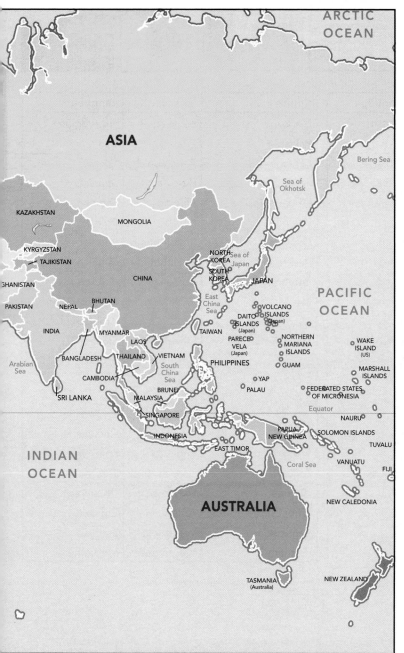

ARCTIC OCEAN

ASIA

Bering Sea

Sea of Okhotsk

KAZAKHSTAN

MONGOLIA

KYRGYZSTAN

TAJIKISTAN

GHANISTAN

CHINA

NORTH KOREA

Sea of Japan

SOUTH KOREA

JAPAN

PACIFIC OCEAN

PAKISTAN

NEPAL

BHUTAN

East China Sea

VOLCANO ISLANDS (Japan)

WAKE ISLAND (US)

INDIA

MYANMAR

TAIWAN

DAITO ISLANDS (Japan)

NORTHERN MARIANA ISLANDS

Arabian Sea

BANGLADESH

LAOS

THAILAND

VIETNAM

PARECE VELA (Japan)

GUAM

CAMBODIA

South China Sea

PHILIPPINES

MARSHALL ISLANDS

SRI LANKA

BRUNEI

YAP

MALAYSIA

PALAU

FEDERATED STATES OF MICRONESIA

SINGAPORE

Equator

NAURU

INDONESIA

PAPUA NEW GUINEA

SOLOMON ISLANDS

INDIAN OCEAN

EAST TIMOR

Coral Sea

TUVALU

VANUATU

FIJI

AUSTRALIA

NEW CALEDONIA

TASMANIA (Australia)

NEW ZEALAND

ATLANTIC OCEAN

FINLAND

NORWAY

SWEDEN

RUSSIA

North Sea

ESTONIA

IRELAND

DENMARK

LATVIA

Baltic Sea

LITHUANIA

UNITED KINGDOM

NETHERLANDS

BELARUS

POLAND

BELGIUM

GERMANY

LUXEMBOURG

CZECH REPUBLIC

UKRAINE

FRANCE

SLOVAKIA

SWITZERLAND

AUSTRIA

HUNGARY

MOLDOVA

SLOVENIA

CROATIA

ROMANIA

PORTUGAL

ANDORRA

BOSNIA and HERZEGOVINA

SERBIA and MONTENEGRO

Black Sea

MONACO

ITALY

BULGARIA

SPAIN

MACEDONIA

ALBANIA

GREECE

TURKEY

Mediterranean Sea

MALTA

CYPRUS

Country	Nationality	Language
Afghanistan	Afghan	Afghan
Argentina	Argentine	Spanish
Australia	Australian	English
Bolivia	Bolivian	Spanish
Brazil	Brazilian	Portuguese
Bulgaria	Bulgarian	Bulgarian
Cambodia	Cambodian	Cambodian
Canada	Canadian	English/French
Chile	Chilean	Spanish
China	Chinese	Chinese
Colombia	Colombian	Spanish
Costa Rica	Costa Rican	Spanish
Cuba	Cuban	Spanish
(The) Czech Republic	Czech	Czech
Denmark	Danish	Danish
(The) Dominican Republic	Dominican	Spanish
Ecuador	Ecuadorian	Spanish
Egypt	Egyptian	Arabic
El Salvador	Salvadorean	Spanish
England	English	English
Estonia	Estonian	Estonian
Ethiopia	Ethiopian	Amharic

Country	Nationality	Language
Finland	Finnish	Finnish
France	French	French
Germany	German	German
Greece	Greek	Greek
Guatemala	Guatemalan	Spanish
Haiti	Haitian	Haitian Kreyol
Honduras	Honduran	Spanish
Hungary	Hungarian	Hungarian
India	Indian	Hindi
Indonesia	Indonesian	Indonesian
Israel	Israeli	Hebrew
Italy	Italian	Italian
Japan	Japanese	Japanese
Jordan	Jordanian	Arabic
Korea	Korean	Korean
Laos	Laotian	Laotian
Latvia	Latvian	Latvian
Lebanon	Lebanese	Arabic
Lithuania	Lithuanian	Lithuanian
Malaysia	Malaysian	Malay
Mexico	Mexican	Spanish
New Zealand	New Zealander	English
Nicaragua	Nicaraguan	Spanish

Country	Nationality	Language
Norway	Norwegian	Norwegian
Pakistan	Pakistani	Urdu
Panama	Panamanian	Spanish
Peru	Peruvian	Spanish
(The) Philippines	Filipino	Tagalog
Poland	Polish	Polish
Portugal	Portuguese	Portuguese
Puerto Rico	Puerto Rican	Spanish
Romania	Romanian	Romanian
Russia	Russian	Russian
Saudi Arabia	Saudi	Arabic
Slovakia	Slovak	Slovak
Spain	Spanish	Spanish
Sweden	Swedish	Swedish
Switzerland	Swiss	German/French/Italian
Taiwan	Taiwanese	Chinese
Thailand	Thai	Thai
Turkey	Turkish	Turkish
Ukraine	Ukrainian	Ukrainian
(The) United States	American	English
Venezuela	Venezuelan	Spanish
Vietnam	Vietnamese	Vietnamese

LISTAS DE VERBOS

Verbos regulares

Los verbos regulares tienen cuatro patrones de deletreo diferentes para el pasado y el participio.

---

1 Hay que añadir **–ed** al final del verbo. Por ejemplo: | act → act**ed**

act	burp	deliver	floss	lower	pour	saute	talk
add	cash	discuss	form	mark	print	scratch	turn
answer	check	dress	grill	match	record	seat	twist
ask	clean	drill	guard	mix	relax	select	vacuum
assist	clear	dust	hand (in)	mow	repair	shorten	vomit
bank	collect	edit	help	open	repeat	sign	walk
boil	comb	end	insert	paint	request	simmer	wash
box	construct	enter	iron	pass (out)	respond	spell	watch
brainstorm	cook	establish	leak	peel	rest	sprain	wax
broil	correct	explain	lengthen	plant	return	steam	work
brush	cough	faint	listen	play	roast	swallow	
burn	cross (out)	fix	look	polish	rock		

---

2 Hay que añadir **–d** al verbo que acaba en **–e**. Por ejemplo: | assemble → assemble**d**

assemble	change	erase	introduce	operate	raise	shave	type
bake	circle	examine	manage	organize	remove	slice	underline
balance	close	exchange	measure	overdose	revise	sneeze	unscramble
barbecue	combine	exercise	microwave	practice	scrape	state	use
bathe	describe	file	move	prepare	serve	supervise	wheeze
bruise	dislocate	gargle	nurse	pronounce	share	translate	wrestle
bubble	enforce	grate					

---

3 Hay que poner consonante final doble y añadir **–ed** al final del verbo. Por ejemplo: | chop → chop**ped**

chop	plan	transfer
mop	stir	

4 Elimine la –y final y añada **–ied** al final del verbo. Por ejemplo: | apply → appl**ied**

apply	dry	stir-fry	try
copy	fry	study	

Verbos irregulares

Los siguientes verbos tienen tiempo pasado y/o participio irregular.

be	was	were		leave	left	left
beat	beat	beaten		let	let	let
bleed	bled	bled		make	made	made
break	broke	broken		meet	met	met
bring	brought	brought		pay	paid	paid
build	built	built		put	put	put
buy	bought	bought		read	read	read
choose	chose	chosen		rewrite	rewrote	rewritten
come	came	come		ring	rang	rung
cut	cut	cut		say	said	said
do	did	done		see	saw	seen
draw	drew	drawn		sell	sold	sold
drink	drank	drunk		set	set	set
drive	drove	driven		sit	sat	sat
eat	ate	eaten		sleep	slept	slept
fall	fell	fallen		speak	spoke	spoken
feed	fed	fed		stand	stood	stood
fly	flew	flown		sweep	swept	swept
get	got	gotten		swim	swam	swum
give	gave	given		take	took	taken
go	went	gone		teach	taught	taught
grow	grew	grown		throw	threw	thrown
have	had	had		understand	understood	understood
hold	held	held		withdraw	withdrew	withdrawn
hurt	hurt	hurt		write	wrote	written

GLOSARIO (INGLÉS)

The bold number indicates the page(s) on which the word appears. The number that follows indicates the word's location in the illustration and in the word list on the page. For example, "address **3**-5" indicates that the word *address* is on page 3 and is item number 5.

carpet **51**-10
carpet sweeper **69**-4
carrot **99**-24
carry-on bag **231**-10
carton **113**-6
cartoon **239**-17
cash **155**-1
cash a check **153**-C
cash machine **153**-12
cash register **111**-6
cashier **111**-9, **205**-14
cast **177**-19
cat food **109**-20
catfish **101**-24
cauliflower **99**-4
cavity **167**-17, **177**-G
CD **149**-12
CD player **149**-13
CD-ROM **151**-5
CD-ROM drive **151**-4
CDs **159**-14
ceiling **47**-11
celery **99**-1
cell phone **149**-25
cell phone number **3**-14
Celsius **33**-21
cement mixer **221**-11
cent **38**
center **195**-21a
Centigrade **33**-21
centimeter **194**-8
central processing unit **151**-2
cereal **107**-1
certified mail **157**-9
chain **139**-7
chair **11**-5, **49**-2
chalk **9**-13
chalkboard **11**-10
chandelier **49**-10
change purse **139**-18

change the baby's diaper **187**-B
change-of-address form **157**-15
changing table **55**-6
cheap **91**-26
check **125**-5, **153**-3, **155**-2
check register **155**-20
check your answers **17**-9
check *your* blood pressure **175**-C
checkbook **155**-19
checked **141**-8
check-in **231**-A
check-in counter **231**-11
checkout counter **111**-5
checkout desk **159**-27
checkout line **111**-4
cheddar cheese **105**-10
cheek **163**-11
cheerleading **191**-6
cheese **103**-6
cheeseburger **119**-2
chef **123**-16, **205**-15
chemicals **203**-16
chemistry **189**-8
cherries **97**-25
cherry picker **221**-16
chess club **191**-16
chest **51**-11, **55**-3, **163**-21
chest of drawers **51**-11, **55**-3
chest pain **167**-24
chest X-ray **175**-H
chicken **101**-12
chicken breasts **101**-13

chicken legs **101**-14
chicken pox **173**-17
chicken salad sandwich **121**-22
chicken sandwich **119**-5
chicken thighs **101**-16
chicken wings **101**-15, **126**-4
chief justice **243**-14
child **85**-1
child day-care worker **205**-16
child-care center **73**-6, **161**-G, **187**-19
child-care worker **161**-17, **187**-20
children **5, 85**-1
children's books **159**-7
Children's Clothing Department **145**-9
children's program **239**-24
children's section **159**-6
chili **119**-12
chili pepper **99**-34
chills **167**-21
chimney **59**-26, **67**-5
chimneysweep **67**-C
chin **163**-18
china **49**-12
china cabinet **49**-11
chocolate cake **127**-24
chocolate milk **103**-4
choir **191**-3
choose the correct answer **17**-11
chop **117**-2
chop up **117**-2
chorus **191**-3

Christmas **247**-9
church **161**-I
circle **195**-21
circle the correct answer **17**-12
circumference **195**-21d
citizen **245**-12
city **3**-9, **45**-13
city hall **81**-7, **161**-D
city manager **161**-9
clams **101**-28
classical music **239**-9
classified ad **61**-1, **217**-3
classroom **21**-E
clean **91**-5, **213**-5
clean the apartment **25**-1
clean the bathroom **69**-H
clean the house **25**-1
clean the wound **177**-A
clean *your* teeth **177**-D
cleaners **73**-7
cleanser **69**-19
clear **33**-3
clear the table **125**-A
clerk **21**-1, **111**-16
clinic **73**-8
clip-on earrings **141**-6
clock **11**-11
clock radio **51**-16, **149**-8
clogged **65**-2
close the wound **177**-B
close your book **13**-14
closed **91**-22

cloth diaper **187**-8
clothing **141**
clothing store **73**-9
cloudy **33**-2
coach **21**-10
coat **133**-1
cockroaches **65**-11e
cocoa **103**-29
coconut **97**-13
coffee **103**-24, **121**-13
coffee pot **49**-6
coffee shop **73**-10
coffee table **47**-22
coffeemaker **53**-27
cold **33**-25, **89**-34, **93**-6, **167**-8
cold tablets **181**-2
cole slaw **105**-12
collar **143**-17
collect the tests **17**-10
cologne **185**-21
colon **197**-14
comb **185**-11
comb *my* hair **23**-9, **185**-H
combine **117**-11
come home **25**-16
comedy **239**-16,23
comedy club **239**-5
comforter **51**-9
comma **197**-11
community service **191**-8
compass directions **229**
computer **11**-7, **151**-1, **203**-2
computer club **191**-14
computer game **151**-22
computer hardware **151**

computer science **189**-11
computer software **151, 159**-16
computer software engineer **205**-17
computer store **73**-11
concert **233**-3, **239**-2
conclusions **203**-F
concrete mixer truck **221**-19
condiments **107**
conditioner **185**-9
condo **45**-5
condominium **45**-5
conductor **225**-18
cone **195**-26
confused **95**-16
congested **169**-5
congressmen **243**-2
congresswomen **243**-2
Constitution **245**-A,3
construct **213**-4
construction worker **205**-18
container **113**-7
convenience store **73**-12
conveyor belt **219**-10
cook **117**-14, **205**-15, **213**-6
cook dinner **23**-17
cookbook **53**-30
cookies **107**-2
cooking oil **107**-25
cool **33**-24
copier **159**-4
copy the word **15**-15
corn **99**-2
corned beef **105**-6
correct your mistakes **15**-4

NÚMEROS, DÍAS DE LA SEMANA, MESES DEL AÑO

Cardinal Numbers

1	one
2	two
3	three
4	four
5	five
6	six
7	seven
8	eight
9	nine
10	ten
11	eleven
12	twelve
13	thirteen
14	fourteen
15	fifteen
16	sixteen
17	seventeen
18	eighteen
19	nineteen
20	twenty
21	twenty–one
22	twenty–two
30	thirty
40	forty
50	fifty
60	sixty
70	seventy
80	eighty
90	ninety
100	one hundred
101	one hundred (and) one
102	one hundred (and) two
1,000	one thousand
10,000	ten thousand
100,000	one hundred thousand
1,000,000	one million
1,000,000,000	one billion

Ordinal Numbers

1st	first
2nd	second
3rd	third
4th	fourth
5th	fifth
6th	sixth
7th	seventh
8th	eighth
9th	ninth
10th	tenth
11th	eleventh
12th	twelfth
13th	thirteenth
14th	fourteenth
15th	fifteenth
16th	sixteenth
17th	seventeenth
18th	eighteenth
19th	nineteenth
20th	twentieth
21st	twenty–first
22nd	twenty–second
30th	thirtieth
40th	fortieth
50th	fiftieth
60th	sixtieth
70th	seventieth
80th	eightieth
90th	ninetieth
100th	one hundredth
101st	one hundred (and) first
102nd	one hundred (and) second
1,000th	one thousandth
10,000th	ten thousandth
100,000th	one hundred thousandth
1,000,000th	one millionth
1,000,000,000th	one billionth

Days of the Week

- Sunday
- Monday
- Tuesday
- Wednesday
- Thursday
- Friday
- Saturday

Months of the Year

- January
- February
- March
- April
- May
- June
- July
- August
- September
- October
- November
- December

THEMATIC INDEX

ÍNDICE TEMÁTICO